M000076648

African Folk Tales

Carol Kruesga Trakler

DOVER · THRIFT · EDITIONS

African Folk Tales

YOTI LANE

WITH DRAWINGS BY
BLAIR HUGHES-STANTON

DOVER PUBLICATIONS, INC.
Mineola, New York

DOVER THRIFT EDITIONS

GENERAL EDITOR: MARY CAROLYN WALDREP
EDITOR OF THIS VOLUME: JANET B. KOPITO

Bibliographical Note

African Folk Tales, first published by Dover Publications, Inc., in 2015, is an unabridged republication of the work originally published by Peter Lunn Publishers Limited, London, in 1946. The illustration plates that appeared in color in that edition are included here as black and white.

International Standard Book Number
ISBN-13: 978-0-486-79198-2
ISBN-10: 0-486-79198-X

Manufactured in the United States by Courier Corporation
79198X01   2015
www.doverpublications.com

Contents

FOREWORD

THESE ARE TALES told round the fires in West Africa when the day's work is done. In their original form they are rather like our operas, as they are told through the medium of music and dancing as well as in words. None of them have been written down before. Some are old, and some are quite modern, because the Africans have new stories just as we have.

I wish to thank Egbert Udo Udomo for providing me with the material for a number of these stories which he heard as a child in Calabar.

YOTI LANE

FOREWORD

To Lynn
who loves animals

African Folk Tales

THE ANIMALS GO TO EARTH

THERE WAS ONCE a wise old tortoise who became very tired of life in the bush. There had been droughts, and quarrels, and feuds ever since he could remember, and the tortoise began to wonder if there was not some peaceful spot to which he could migrate with his family. He was sitting on the river bank when the hare came by and stopped to chat.

"I had a very curious adventure this morning," said the hare.

"What happened to you?" asked the tortoise.

"I noticed a hole under the roots of that big tree near where the palm nuts grow. I went down it, and found myself in a tunnel. I went a very long way, and still didn't reach the end. I thought it wiser to return as I was alone, but I believe that tunnel leads somewhere."

"That's interesting," said the tortoise. "If you care to come back and explore I'll go with you."

The hare looked a bit doubtful. His only means of defending himself was to run away as fast as he could if any danger arose. The tortoise on the other hand could protect himself but he couldn't protect any one else, and anything might happen in this strange tunnel. Then the hare remembered the mongoose. The mongoose usually has a sweet and gentle disposition, but he can put up a good fight if he is provoked.

"I'll go back, if I may bring the mongoose along. He's a useful fellow in trouble," replied the hare.

"All right," said the tortoise. "You go get him, and I'll meet you both at the foot of the tree."

So the tortoise set off at a stately pace, and the hare loped away through the bush to find the mongoose. He went a long way before he heard the queer squeaky, chirruping voice of his friend.

1

The mongoose and his wife were having a lunch of bananas. The hare told them of his strange discovery, and suggested that the mongoose should come and explore the tunnel.

"If you go I'm coming also," announced Mrs. Mongoose.

"But it may be dangerous," said her husband.

"I don't mind that, you know I hate being left alone," she replied. Her husband knew this to be true. No mongoose likes to be alone. They are very friendly, lovable creatures, and pine away unless they have company.

"All right, come along then, but don't say I didn't warn you if we run into trouble!"

So off they went, keeping up with the hare without much difficulty, despite their short legs.

They reached the tree just as the tortoise arrived, and the hare pointed out the opening of the tunnel. The mongoose went first, the hare second, the tortoise followed, and Mrs. Mongoose brought up in the rear, the idea being that if anything followed them down the tunnel she would make good use of her teeth and claws. Down, and down they went. They were all a little nervous but no one liked to admit it. Finally the tunnel became steep, and they lost their footing, and tumbled down one after the other, until they slid into a brightly lighted place.

They found themselves in a beautiful valley, well wooded, and with a river running through it. There was no sound of any living thing. Hastily scuttling into the shade of a large tree they took council.

"We seem to be in another world," exclaimed Mrs. Mongoose.

"But how can we be in another world when we haven't died?" asked the hare.

"Be reasonable, friends," hissed the tortoise. "This is simply some hidden valley that no one has discovered. Or perhaps they have. It doesn't mean nobody is here because we can't see them at this moment."

"You mean spirits?" squeaked the hare.

"Of course I don't, but if people are here they might have heard us coming, and now be hiding, just as we are. Hare, you had better scout round while we stay here. Come back and report if you can see anyone."

So the hare set off, running from shadow to shade, and listening and watching intently, but he heard nothing but the rustle of leaves, and the gentle gurgle of the stream, and he saw nothing, but

trees, and grass, and flowers, and vegetation that made his mouth water. After he had made a long detour he returned to his friends.

"The place seems like a dream," he told them.

"But it's quite deserted. There isn't an animal, or a bird, or even an insect."

"And no men?" asked Mrs. Mongoose.

"No, certainly no men. I couldn't have failed to see them."

After this there was a long silence while everyone did some thinking.

"You know," said the tortoise at last, "it's curious you should have found this place today, because only this morning I was reflecting how nice it would be to go somewhere where life was always pleasant and peaceful. This certainly seems to be so."

"I have never seen so much food," said the hare.

"It's a beautiful place to bring up a family," Mrs. Mongoose squeaked wistfully.

"It's a great improvement on where we've come from," her husband agreed. ,

"Do you propose we stay here?" asked the hare.

"I think we should try it. There may be some danger we know nothing about of course, but it's worth the risk," replied the tortoise.

"But won't it be lonely?" asked Mrs. Mongoose. "Just us four in this vast place."

"I would of course bring my family—at least some members of it," said the tortoise.

"So should I," said the hare.

"But if we let everyone in," said the mongoose. "won't the place soon become as full of troubles as the world we have left. You know some mongooses are quarrelsome most of the time."

"And there are our enemies the snakes," his wife reminded him. "I get so tired having to kill snakes, but everyone expects us to do it. Now if we lived in a place where there were no snakes I could be so happy."

"If I lived in a place where there were no snares *I* could be so happy," put in the hare.

"We had better draw up a list and decide just whom we shall allow here," said the tortoise.

"But how can we keep the others out if the news gets round."

"This place is very well hidden," said the hare. "We must see that the news doesn't get round. We shall only tell people we can trust, and they will have to agree to come with us right away. They must not be given a chance to talk to anyone else. Then we shall lead them into the glade above, blindfold them, and bring them down the tunnel. Once here they must never return to the world above."

"I'm sure they wouldn't want to," exclaimed Mrs. Mongoose. "I for one am prepared to stay here for ever."

"Then," said the tortoise, "we had better decide now whom we shall have here."

"I feel that my people have a big claim," said the mongoose. "Ever since we can remember we have been hunted and trapped by man. Our numbers are declining rapidly, and soon we shall have vanished unless man stops his stupid habit of trying to catch us, and hunt us. We are harmless, quiet people. We only destroy snakes when they get in our way."

"That is true," said the tortoise. "We grant that your people have a big claim. I leave it to your discretion to pick the best ones and bring them here."

"I feel we hares have a big claim too."

"I'm not too sure," said the tortoise. "You have very large families, and you eat recklessly. Not even this valley could support a large number of hares. No, you must bring only a few, and you must make it clear that they can't eat recklessly. If they want to do that they had better stay in the upper world."

"All right," agreed the hare. "I'll only bring the ones who are prepared to abide by the rules."

"As regards my own folk," went on the tortoise. "They don't take to new ways, and they won't care to move. A few of the young, and enterprising ones will come, but that's all."

"But we'll want more people than that," said Mrs. Mongoose. "Who else shall we have?"

"We don't want animals who kill and eat each other, and we don't want people with nasty dispositions," said the hare firmly.

"I agree," said the mongoose. "The buffalo, the lions, the leopard, and the crocodile are definitely out."

"I agree," said the hare. "Now what about the bush pigs. They have their points, you know."

"They are very unsociable," wheezed Mrs. Mongoose.

"Suppose we leave them aside for the time being," suggested the tortoise. "I propose we let some deer in; a few of each species."

This was passed unanimously.

"And the zebra," put in the hare. "I know they aren't sociable either, but no one is better at sensing danger, or intruders, and they are quite harmless."

"All right, a few zebra," conceded Mrs. Mongoose.

"That goes for the giraffe also," said the mongoose. So they decided to have a giraffe family.

"No jackals, no hyenas, no vultures," said the hare firmly, and everyone agreed.

"What about birds?" asked Mrs. Mongoose.

"We'd better make a separate list of them," said the tortoise. "There are so many varieties." So this was agreed.

"What about the monkeys?" asked the mongoose.

At this everyone talked at once. There was a most serious division of opinion on monkeys. The tortoise believed that there were good, bad and indifferent monkeys. The mongoose considered all of them mischievous and greedy. Mrs. Mongoose had some great friends among certain species, but disliked nearly all the others. The hare believed monkeys were not to be trusted. In the end it was decided that a few monkeys might be admitted on their own merits.

After this exhausting discussion the four had a good meal and a rest.

"Oh dear, I wish I didn't have to go up that tunnel again," said Mrs. Mongoose.

"Well, you needn't," said the tortoise. "You and your husband may stay here. Hare will take messages, and bring the first batch of your relatives here tomorrow."

"That's very decent of you," said the mongoose. "We'll be glad to stay."

"Be cautious," the hare warned them. "Keep very quiet." "You can rely on us," said the mongoose. "We'll make no move until you return."

So off went the hare and the tortoise up the tunnel, and hare went off further still as soon as they reached the top, so that by evening he had taken many messages, and people began to come from all over the bush to talk to the tortoise.

It was surprising how few of them really were willing to set off on an adventure to a new country. The old deer, robust creatures, were willing to take a chance, and some of their young sons were of like mind, but the female deer needed a good deal of persuasion from their husbands and sons. The mongooses who are inquisitive creatures were willing, but only a few of the tortoises wanted to move. However a small band was eventually got together, and very early next morning they met in the glade near the big tree. There the hare bound their eyes, and leading the mongooses, made his way down the tunnel. As soon as he arrived at the bottom he saw the two mongooses who had stayed waiting eagerly.

They helped to untie the bandages from the eyes of their relatives, and they all set up an absolute babel of exclamations, greetings, and mutual enthusiasm.

"How did you pass the night?" asked the hare.

"Well, naturally we didn't sleep much, I watched and listened most of the time, but there were no strange sounds. I'm quite sure no one lives here," said the mongoose.

"Very well," said the hare. "I'll go back, and fetch some more people. You look after your relatives and get them settled down comfortably."

So back he went for the deer.

Of course, the disappearance of a number of people soon began to arouse great interest in the bush. The monkeys in particular were almost out of their minds with curiosity. But the tortoise had very wisely decided that even the monkeys who were to be allowed to come down should be the very last to be told anything, so that they would not be tempted to chatter. The leopard also gave them trouble, because he was abroad both in daylight and at night, and he moved noiselessly, and was very cunning. On several occasions whole bands of selected candidates had to be sent home because they found the leopard had trailed them.

The crocodile also got wind of something strange and came to see the tortoise in order to try and gain information.

"You seem to be very busy lately," he said. "You are scarcely ever at home."

"It's a busy time of year," replied the tortoise.

"Is it?" asked the crocodile. "I wondered if you were thinking of moving?"

"I may," said the tortoise. "I should be glad of a change."

"Indeed, and where were you thinking of going?" asked the crocodile.

"Some distance from here," answered the tortoise.

"You know I'll miss you if you go," said the crocodile. "We've been neighbours for so many years. I've half a mind to come along."

"I don't think you'd like it," the tortoise told him. "The place I'm moving to is a sort of settlement, and we are all vegetable eaters. You would probably become flatulent on our diet."

"Oh, I don't know," replied the crocodile. "I expect I'd find a bit of meat somehow."

"That's what I was afraid of," said the tortoise.

The crocodile lashed his tail.

"What are you suggesting?" he cried.

"Nothing," said the tortoise pacifically. "Nothing at all." With that he closed his eyes and pretended to doze. This was an old trick which never failed to irritate the crocodile. He snapped his jaws angrily, and wished for the thousandth time that the tortoise hadn't got a shell that not even a crocodile could digest.

At last the animals who had been approached, and decided to migrate, all moved down to the new settlement.

"It's strange," remarked the hare. "How few came really, yet practically all of them used to complain about the life in the bush."

"That's their nature," the tortoise reminded him. "Most people like grousing but few of them have the courage to make a change."

"Shall we allow any more to come down in future?" asked the hare.

"A few unusual ones, but they will have to wait till they're asked."

"What if someone comes down by accident?" asked the hare.

"Unless we know them very well, and can vouch for them being suitable, we can't let them stay. This place is too tempting, and we should have no law and order if the wrong people got in."

"When are you moving down?" asked the hare.

The tortoise sighed.

"I'm not sure that I shall ever move down permanently. You see so many of our people are rather foolish. I think I'll have to stay and keep an eye on them. If the crocodile and the leopard got too much of their own way I don't know what would happen."

"I don't see why you should bother about other people," the hare shrilled.

"I couldn't be comfortable if I didn't," the tortoise replied. "We are the lucky ones down here, but we must not forget about the others in the world above."

"A lot of thanks you'll get," scoffed the hare.

"That doesn't matter," said the tortoise, and turned away, and started slowly up the tunnel.

Years passed, and still the tortoise divided his time between the upper and the lower world.

In the lower world all was peace and quiet, and everyone had enough to eat. None of the selected animals of the lower world were ambitious people like those above. In the bush the lion roared that he was King. The leopard snarled warning that he was Lord of his domain. The crocodile slew ruthlessly in order to create terror. The animals who were strong in tooth and claw bullied their neighbours, and the more helpless ones relied on flight to save them.

"It's a great life," a young leopard told the tortoise. "At least it is for me. I can fight anything in the forest. I live gloriously."

"I only hope you will die as gloriously," replied the tortoise.

"Oh, you are just a defeatist," snarled the young leopard and stalked off flicking his whiskers.

This sort of thing made the tortoise unhappy. He went about talking to all the animals, and trying to persuade them to live at peace with each other. But it was no use. Either they were bullies, or they were bullied, and they simply could not imagine any other mode of existence. So the tortoise scarcely ever found any suitable recruits for the colony in the underworld.

"Why worry about them?" asked the hare.

"Because there are signs and omens that a great drought is coming. They will perish in large numbers, and the very bush itself may die. If a fire were started now it would burn like tinder. I would like to save some of them before it is too late."

In due time the drought came, and the fire as well, and all the animals who had been fighting and preying on each other were driven into a common effort to save themselves. The lion and the hare fled side by side, the leopard ran at the heels of the deer, and was too frightened to attempt a kill. The young leopard who had boasted to the tortoise was trapped and burnt by the fire.

A few refugees found their way down the hole. A small pig or two, and some porcupines, and a whole lot of harmless small animals who were allowed to remain. They interfered with nobody, but seemed too dazed to realise their good fortune.

At length the rains came to the upper world, and put out the fire. But large tracts of bush would not grow again for years, and the survivors who crept back to their old haunts did not have a very happy life.

"Well," said the hare to the tortoise, "I hope you have now abandoned any idea of helping those people up above. You must see now that you are just wasting your time!"

The tortoise shook his head.

"There may be one or two, somewhere, at some time. I prefer to go back."

So back he went, travelling around, looking for a few people who were worthy of a better world. He is still doing it to this day, as doubtless you know if you've ever owned a tortoise. They appear and disappear for long periods in the most mysterious way.

THE QUEST FOR THE IVORY HORN

ONCE UPON A time a King had two sons. He was a very jealous King, jealous even of his eldest son, because he was heir. He also disliked the boy because he was brave, and careless, and popular with the people. This had a bad effect on the boy, who was inclined to defy his father, and to become reckless and adventurous. This made the young Prince even more popular with the people, and the better they liked him the less his father liked him. The old King would have preferred that the younger son had been the heir, because he was delicate and timid, and unlikely to ever be a great man.

At length the old King became so jealous of his heir that he determined to send him on a mission that could only end in his death.

At this time there was war throughout the land, for the old King believed that the best way to be powerful was to have all the neighbouring states fighting with each other, and he intrigued until this came about. Far away from his own country was a small State ruled by the old King. Here, in a strongly armoured fort, was the King's most precious possession, an ancient horn of ivory, which meant as much to the King, as the Crown does to the English monarch.

So the King sent for the Prince, and said, "With all this strife going on I am afraid to keep my horn in such a distant State. I want you to go and bring it here. It will be a difficult and dangerous task,

11

but it is fitting that you, as my heir, should carry it out. If you are afraid of course, I'll go myself."

Even if the young Prince hadn't been brave and full of self-confidence, the mere suggestion that he might be afraid of anything would have driven him on. "Of course I'll go," he told his father. "Don't forget, it's very dangerous," the old man warned him. "Nothing will happen to me!" retorted the Prince, and went off to make his preparations for the journey.

Although the Prince had no fears, the people had. Several wise old men tried to dissuade him, telling him that apart from all the dangers from savage animals, and marauding soldiers, that the King was undoubtedly plotting against him. The Prince was very angry at this, however, and it only made him more determined to get the horn.

The only precaution he took was to go and talk to the oldest woman in the village before he set out. The old lady also warned him, and begged him to take her advice. "When you go to the stable tomorrow morning," she said, "you will find a white horse there. Take him, and take no other. Let the horse guide you. He will take you to a crossroads, and when you get there, use this!" She handed the Prince a white wand. "Hold it up and it will point the way, and follow whither it points."

The Prince humoured the old lady by promising to do what she asked. "Is that all?" he enquired. The old lady shook her head. "No. Your father plans to kill you. At nightfall tomorrow night you will be offered shelter in a certain house, and at midnight it will be burned down. Tie your horse up well away from the house, and only pretend to sleep, and keep the wand in your hand."

The Prince was not inclined to take all this seriously, but he thanked the old lady and went home. Next morning when he went to the stable right enough he found a beautiful white horse he had never seen before. The Prince was very pleased with this and rode away on it, and because he didn't want to hurt the old woman's feelings he was also careful to carry the wand.

As he began to ride he was surprised to find that the horse was indeed setting off in a very determined fashion as if it knew every inch of the road, and so he let it have its way. At length it came to a crossroads and stopped. Out of curiosity the Prince held up the wand. It twisted in his hands as if it were alive, and pointed to a road going due west, so the Prince followed this road.

Just before the sun set he came to a clearing where a number of houses were standing, and a group of people rushed out to greet him enthusiastically. By this time the Prince had begun to believe that the old lady had told him the truth, so he left his horse some distance away, and went to bed with the wand in his hand. Despite the warning that the house would be set on fire, the Prince slept, but after he had been asleep some time he was awakened by the wand twisting around wildly, and he smelled smoke, so he got up and rushed out. From a safe distance he watched the house burn down, and then went to seek his horse, and spent the remainder of the night by its side.

In the morning he heard a great hubbub in the village, so he mounted his horse and rode back. The people pretended to be delighted to hear that he had escaped, but the Prince spoke little and went on his way.

Later in the day they came to the banks of a stream, and the horse, as if sensing danger, refused to cross. But the Prince decided that they must go on, so he flicked the horse with the wand, and it leapt the stream. The Prince soon found that the area was infested by savage animals, and reptiles, but no matter how savage the animals were, as soon as they caught sight of the wand in his hand, they turned tail and fled.

At length he came upon a huge boa constrictor, coiled right in his path. The great snake saw the wand, and made no move to attack, but he gazed at the Prince curiously, and then spoke. "Why do you come this way?" he asked.

The Prince explained that he had been sent on a mission by his father, and that he was determined to accomplish it. He told how the old woman had given him the wand, how she had prophesied that the house would be burned down, and how he would escape, and that he had done so. The boa constrictor listened with great interest.

"It is an evil thing that your father, the King, should rule in such a way, and that he should cause wars. Why do humans want wars, it isn't as if they were hungry and wanted to eat each other, is it?" The Prince said it was not. "Then it is all foolish and evil," the boa constrictor said. "When we kill, we kill to eat. I hope you get the horn, and I hope you become a wise and great King. Go on your way with my blessing."

So the Prince rode on. After a while he became aware that a leopard was trailing him, so curious to see what would happen, he drew up and waited until the leopard came in sight. "What are you doing in my territory?" the leopard asked angrily.

The Prince repeated his story, and found that the leopard, like the snake was sympathetic. He offered a good deal of useful advice about the journey, and told the Prince that by nightfall he would come to the fort that was his destination. So the Prince bade the leopard a polite farewell, and rode on.

As the sun set, he saw a huge fort looming up in the distance, and pulled up his horse to study the place.

He soon realised that any hope he had of getting in by any ordinary means was in vain. The place was teeming with soldiers, and they were obviously on the alert as if expecting someone, and he was afraid there was a hot reception waiting for him. At the same time he was determined that he was going to get the ivory horn, even at the risk of his life.

He was startled to hear a voice beside him. "Welcome King that Shall Be," it said. At his horse's head stood an old wrinkled woman. "Why do you call me 'King that Shall Be?'" he asked. "I have heard from your friend," she replied, "and am here to help you." At this the Prince was amazed. "What friend?" he enquired. The woman named the old lady who had given him the wand. "Tonight when they are asleep, you must follow me. Carry your wand, and I shall lead you to the place where the horn is."

The Prince agreed. He knew he was risking his life, because even if the old lady led him safely into the fort, and he got the horn, it was scarcely likely they would let him get away once the loss was discovered. So he thanked the old lady, and she hid him in the forest till nightfall.

When it was quite dark she came back, and told him to follow her. They moved like ghosts, slipping towards the back of the fort, then through a secret door hidden by trees, and along great underground passages, past rooms full of sleeping soldiers. At length they came to a huge chamber, and on a great table stood a wonderful ivory horn.

"Raise it to your lips, and blow," whispered the old woman.

"But that would be madness," the Prince protested.

"Do as I say," the old woman said quickly. Deciding that this was the most insane thing he had ever done in his life, he raised the horn to his lips, and blew.

The sound seemed to hit the roof and run down all the corridors, echoing like the shouts of a multitude. From all over the fort came the soldiers, crowding into the room. Brave as he was the Prince gave himself up for lost, but he was amazed to see that the old woman by his side was smiling.

"They won't hurt you now you have the horn," she said, "Listen!" The soldiers were all shouting, shouting "Long Live the King!"

It was indeed true, for the old King had learned that the Prince had escaped safely from the fire, and that he had not been molested by the animals, and that he had a magic wand, and he had been so incensed that he died of rage.

Because the Prince had been so brave, and because he held the horn which they all regarded with reverence and awe, the warring peoples allowed him to leave in safety and make his way back to his own country without harm. And the Prince became a very wise and generous King, and he conciliated all tribes, and there has been no war in all that country from that day to this.

THE LOST SISTER

ZARA CROUCHED ON the edge of the bush and looked out at the town, and at the great house where her sister lived. She had found her sister Mizpah at last. It was six years since she had seen her and so much had happened. They had been carrying water from the stream, Zara nine years old, a funny looking little girl with big eyes, and a very thin face and body. No one thought her pretty but everyone admired her elder sister Mizpah. Everyone foretold a wonderful marriage for Mizpah. Surely so beautiful a girl must marry a most important man. Her mother was so proud of her eldest child, she was the favourite of everyone.

Zara remembered how happy they had been that day as they carried the water. They were having a feast, the food had been gathered in, and the whole village was preparing to rejoice. Then, like a clap of thunder came the slavers. One moment the village was happy in the sunshine as the girls carried their water jars, and the next it was full of shrieking, shouting figures. The girls stood and gaped, and then before they could make any move, they found themselves surrounded. Zara remembered very little of what happened after, there was fighting and bloodshed, but she and her sister had been dragged into a hut, bound and thrown to the ground. That evening the slavers set forth with their captives, and for many weary days and nights they marched with but a little rest during the hottest hours of the day, until they came to a large town. Here they were chained in a hut.

"Suppose we are separated?" sobbed Zara. "You are very beautiful and someone is sure to buy you and carry you off, maybe to live in a great Court, but who will want me, small and ugly as I am?"

Mizpah hastily dragged off a charm that she wore round her neck.

"Take this," she told Zara. "If we are separated I will try and get word to you somehow, and no matter what happens some day you must escape and try to find me. Wear this charm so that I may know you because if years pass you will grow up and change. But no matter what happens I shall never cease to try and trace you, my beloved sister."

Next morning Zara's worst fears were fulfilled. They were taken to the slave market, and many eager bidders competed to buy Mizpah. Finally, she was led away by a grim, distinguished looking old man. "He buys slaves for the Sultan of a country far to the North. Mizpah is fortunate, she may become a favourite!" a fellow captive whispered to Zara.

"Oh, if only he had bought me also," Zara whispered.

Her neighbour laughed shortly.

"He only buys the most beautiful girls!"

Zara hid her face in her hands and wept. The selling went on, and finally towards the end Zara was bought by an old man who was a carpet weaver. She soon realised that she might have fallen into worse hands. The old man had a number of slaves of all ages. They had to work hard, but they were not badly treated. Zara soon became a skilful weaver.

One day a dealer from the North came to the market with a strange story. Zara never missed an opportunity of going to the market because it was there that news was circulated, and one day she felt sure she would hear news of Mizpah. Now at last her patience was rewarded. The slave, Mizpah, the dealer said, had been married to the son of the Sultan, and the whole countryside was agog with excitement. It was rare indeed for a slave to have such honour conferred on her. It was of course because she had such great beauty and such a sweet disposition. Very cautiously Zara tried to find out how to get to this far place where her sister lived. The journey would take many months even if she should succeed in escaping. That would be difficult, and the penalty for failure would be death. It would have been easier if poor Zara had money or jewels to bribe someone to help her, but she had nothing, and must depend on her wits.

During the next few weeks she managed to hide away some food, and then one night, when everyone slept she crept out with her small bundle. It took a long time to escape unseen, because people seemed astir all over the place as they usually are in busy towns, but when Zara finally gained the open country she was pretty sure that she had not been seen. The first gleam of daylight found her far in the bush, where she hid in the branches of a great tree. She was terrified that she might go asleep and fall to the ground, so she forced herself to keep awake.

She was not surprised some hours later when she heard two men on the path some distance away. They were talking about an escaped slave.

"She will not get far. Hunger will drive her back, because for one thing no one would dare to help her," one man said to the other. Zara looked anxiously at her bundle of food. She must eat very little. She could eke it out with roots, and berries. Now dozing, now waking, she waited till darkness fell, and then set off in what she judged to be a northern direction.

For days she travelled in this way, growing ever more hungry as her store of food vanished. Finally she felt a little safer, surely she must be too far away for the tale of her escape to be known to the people around.

That night she came to a great lake, with many boats and fishermen. Taking her courage in her hands she approached one of the men and asked him if he would take her across the lake. "Who are you?" he asked suspiciously. "I wish to visit my married sister who lives on the other side of the lake, and wishes me to go to her." "Have you money?" asked the boatman. "No," replied Zara, "but my sister has much money, and I promise you that a reward will be sent to you if only you will trust me." The man looked glum. "Oh well," he said at last. "I'm going anyhow, so I suppose I've nothing to lose by taking you." "I promise you you can't lose, but you may not hear from me for some time," Zara said. "Hm, you sound honest!" the man commented. "Get in, but you'll have to make yourself useful."

They reached the other side of the lake next day, and Zara set off once more. She was very glad that she had the charm her sister had given her because it was three years since they had separated, and Zara knew she had grown much taller. Apart from that she had no idea how she looked, for she had never seen a mirror, during all the time she had been a slave.

That evening Zara came to a village, and the people were kind, and gave her food and shelter, but to her dismay she learned that the town where her sister lived was many weeks journey away. It was months, however, not weeks, before Zara reached the place, because as she had no money or food she had to earn a living as she went along.

Now at last she had come to the town, and sat on the edge of the bush and looked at the lights, wondering how she would manage to make herself known to her sister.

Now although Zara was unaware of the fact, Mizpah had made such efforts to find her that the story of the lost sister was generally known, and a dishonest tailor and his brother who was a merchant, and who lived some distance from the town, had decided to put a very wicked plan into action. The merchant had a young daughter of Zara's age, who seemed to tally with the description Mizpah had given of her sister. "She is small and thin with big eyes, and she wears a charm in the form of a tortoise which I gave her." Now the merchant's daughter was small and thin with big eyes, and she was also clever and cunning. Her father and uncle had no doubt that with their help she could pretend to be Zara, and reap all the benefits to be gained from being sister of Mizpah. The only thing lacking was the charm. It had to be identical with the one Mizpah had given Zara, and so far they had not managed to find a suitable one.

On the evening when Zara reached the outskirts of the town, the tailor was returning from a visit to his brother. He was an inquisitive fellow, and seeing a stranger sitting by the roadside he paused and asked if he could help her. He seemed so kind and friendly that Zara poured out her story, and the tailor almost beside himself because of the chance Fate had thrown in his way, did his best to conceal his elation.

"This is an extraordinary story," he told Zara. "I am willing to help you, but you can't blame me for wanting more information." Then he proceeded to ply her with questions until he had all sorts of details about the girl's home life, their relatives, in fact everything he needed to enable his niece to make good her claim that she was really the lost sister.

At length he had sufficient, and he pretended to pause and consider. "I am convinced you are telling me the truth," he said at last. "But there are great difficulties ahead of you. It is very difficult to see your sister. You must remember she is a very important person. Also there are dangers. If your story were known evil people might try to steal the charm and put you out of the way. Now here is what I suggest. Down the road there lives a blacksmith and his wife. They are kind people, and if you go along and ask for food and shelter they will give it to you. But don't give them your real name, or tell them your story. In the meanwhile I'll take the charm to your sister. I have influence, and I shall be able to gain admission to her, and tomorrow evening I shall come and fetch you."

Poor Zara was torn by indecision. She hated parting with the charm, but she knew she would have great difficulty in obtaining an interview with Mizpah. At length, persuaded by the cunning arguments of the tailor, she agreed to his scheme, handed over the charm and set off down the road to the house of the blacksmith.

As soon as the tailor had the charm he ran off as fast as he could back to the house of his brother. There he told the great news to the merchant and his daughter, and coached the girl in the story of Zara's life until she knew it as well as a clever actress knows her part in a play.

Then he travelled back through the night with the merchant and the girl, and as they travelled they concocted a story to explain how "Zara" had arrived in the town.

Next morning, by dint of bribery, the merchant secured an interview with Mizpah on pretence of showing her some very beautiful materials.

As soon as he was in her presence he spread a piece of cloth, and palming the charm, saw to it that her eyes fell on it, at the same time motioning her to secrecy.

For a moment Mizpah turned deadly pale, and then commanded her maids' to leave her.

"Where did you get that?" she gasped as soon as she was alone with the merchant.

"From your sister. On my way home two days ago I found a young girl who had fallen exhausted by the wayside. I took her to my home, and when she recovered she told me who she was, and that she wanted to see you."

"Where is she?" asked Mizpah eagerly.

"Waiting outside," said the merchant.

"Bring her in quickly. Oh my sister, my dear little sister, is found. My prayers have been answered," Mizpah sobbed, overcome with emotion.

Within a few minutes the false Zara was ushered in. Well coached, she ran to her sister, and threw herself at her feet. Weeping, Mizpah raised the girl in her arms, and poured out questions, all of which "Zara" was able to answer. The merchant was delighted at the good performance his daughter was putting on. No one could have done better.

Then Mizpah sent for her husband, and told him her lost sister was found. The young man was almost as overjoyed as his wife, and they did everything in their power to make the girl happy, and comfortable, so that she would forget past unhappiness.

She was fed on delicious food, bathed in perfumed water, and dressed in beautiful garments. A great feast was prepared to celebrate the reunion of the sisters.

Meanwhile the real Zara waited in the home of the blacksmith, and became more and more anxious. Her hosts were at a loss to comfort her because they did not know her story, and while they were wondering about her trouble, a neighbour arrived with the amazing news of the recovering of Mizpah's lost sister. They were completely bewildered when their mysterious guest, who was also listening, suddenly gave a great cry, and fell to the ground unconscious. She was ill for many days afterwards, and as she began to recover Zara tried to make plans. She realised the dishonest tailor had tricked her, and that without the charm she was helpless. But she was a clever girl, and brave, and as she got better she made plans. She told the kind blacksmith that she wanted above all things to work in the palace. So when she was quite well the blacksmith approached a cousin who was a kitchen hand, and obtained work for Zara at the same humble tasks.

Zara was clever and willing, and resolved to work her way up so that eventually she would come in contact with her sister, and the mysterious girl who was impersonating herself. As the weeks passed, tales began to circulate about the impostor. It was said that she was taking advantage of her position, was bad tempered, arrogant and greedy. That she had wheedled large sums of money out of Mizpah and her husband, and also jewellery, and that people were beginning to dislike her.

Months passed. Still the impostor held her place, although she became more and more unpopular, and Mizpah more and more troubled at the character of her sister. In the meanwhile Zara made steady progress, and was now a sewing woman, and frequently saw Mizpah, and had spoken to her.

"You are very pretty you know," Mizpah said to her one day. Zara jumped.

"Pretty? I've never been pretty," she exclaimed.

"But you are. Don't you ever look in a mirror?" Mizpah asked.

"No, I never bother. I was always very plain as a child, and I can't believe I'll ever be pretty now."

"What age are you?" Mizpah asked.

"Fifteen!"

"Just the same age as my sister," Mizpah said softly, and with a sigh, turned and went away.

About that time there came exciting developments for the impostor. An important man from further north was extremely desirous of making a wealthy and influential marriage for his son. He accordingly approached Mizpah's husband to sound him out on the prospects of a marriage with Zara. Now if Zara had been the sweet and charming person Mizpah had described in the past, this idea would have borne no fruit, but as it was the husband saw it as a possible solution to a very painful situation. By this time Zara's bad temper, arrogance and selfishness were notorious. Also her demands for clothes, money and jewellery seemed endless. The truth was, of course, that the impostor's father and uncle were constantly urging her to make these demands, which she was compelled to do. Mizpah was dreadfully unhappy, even though she did not know half the painful truths about Zara's rapacity, and all she could say in her sister's defence was that the years of cruel slavery had affected her character, and that she would improve in time. But neither Mizpah nor anyone else could detect the slightest sign of improvement.

So Mizpah's husband went to his wife with every determination to be firm. He told her of the marriage offer, and said he must demand that it be acceded to, as he was not prepared to keep Zara in his home much longer. At first Mizpah wept because her lost sister was to be taken from her so soon, but in the end she had to admit that the marriage seemed the best way out for everyone.

"But what of the young man?" she asked. "It seems unfair that he should have this burden thrust upon him."

"I shall give a good marriage portion," said the husband. "I shall be glad to do so, and rid myself of further extortions."

So he returned to the father, sealed the marriage bargain, and the old man went back to his son. At first the son was angry. "I am quite well aware that you desire me to marry, but I object to all these arrangements being made behind my back. We are not poor, and I have no reason to marry for money. How do you know I shall like this girl?"

"Is she not the sister of Mizpah who is famed for her great beauty, and sweetness of disposition? Why you might search the world and not find such a bride. You should be grateful to me for my wisdom and good luck in securing the girl for you."

Nevertheless it took some time to convince the young man, but in the end the father succeeded, and plans went ahead.

Zara was busy sewing from morning until night, and she was nearly ill with worry over what had happened. She knew that a large marriage settlement would be made on the impostor, and once the marriage took place it would matter little what happened. She would be no longer in daily contact with Mizpah and would never be exposed, and the real Zara would have even less hope than before of unmasking the culprits.

So matters continued until the eve of the wedding, which was to be a great event. That evening Zara went to visit her old friend the blacksmith, and was amazed when she walked into their house to find the fisherman who had taken her across the lake a year ago.

They gazed at each other in astonishment.

"What are you doing here?" demanded the fisherman.

"This is a very great friend of ours," explained the wife of the blacksmith.

"But she's the person I've come to seek—the lost sister—the one who broke her word, and never paid me for helping her," shouted the fisherman.

At that everyone started to talk at once, and it was some minutes before Zara, who realised that the whole truth must now be told, could make herself heard. It was a long story, and when she had finished they gaped at her in amazement.

"You do recognise me, don't you?" she asked the fisherman. "And you do remember the charm I wore round my neck?"

"Of course I remember it," replied the fisherman. "When I heard the story later, that was how I knew who you were. I trusted you, and I was sure you would not forget me. Then I began to hear how you—I mean the other one—were greedy and selfish, and I then resolved that I was going to get my rights because but for me helping you, you—I mean the other one—but of course it was really you." The fisherman paused, completely muddled in his attempts to explain.

"I understand," Zara told him. "It is wonderful that you came because now at last the truth can be made known."

"I wonder who the false Zara can be?" exclaimed the fisherman.

"I think I can guess," said the wife of the blacksmith. "I know who that tailor must be. I've seen him pass here many times, also his brother the merchant. Now I know they are an unscrupulous family, and I know the brother had a daughter about the same age as Zara. I believe she is the impostor!"

"The important thing is to expose her as quickly as possible," said the blacksmith. He turned to Zara. "You must see the husband of your sister. We will come with you and support what you say. Let us go at once!"

So off they went, and Zara hid her three friends in a small room that was seldom used, and slipped off to try and waylay the Prince. As an excuse she carried a cloak she had recently mended. Fortunately there was such fuss and excitement that no one paid much attention to the humble little sewing girl, and she was able to creep into the Prince's room and throw herself at his feet.

"Who are you, what do you want?" he exclaimed.

Zara took her courage in her hands.

"I have evidence to prove that your sister-in-law is an impostor!" she said calmly.

The Prince rose to his feet in astonishment.

"Please hear me," Zara implored him. "Bar the door that we may not be interrupted, because I have a long story to tell."

Curious, the Prince did so, and commanded her to speak.

When she had finished he looked at her searchingly.

"This fisherman, where is he?" he enquired.

"Waiting to speak with you, so are the blacksmith and his wife."

"I'll send a guard for them at once!"

When the trio came in they told everything they knew about Zara, and the Prince felt that there was every possibility that the story was true. It also helped to explain something that had puzzled him so much, the complete difference in disposition between the girl Mizpah had talked of, and the character of the girl who had claimed to be the lost sister.

"I shall have to try and make her admit the fraud. I have an idea. Wait here!"

He hurried in search of his wife.

"I want you to do something and ask no questions," he told her. "I want you to go in search of your sister, and when you find her, talk about old times. Ask her if she remembers how your uncle had a splendid marriage feast. How you had a wonderful red robe, and she had a beautiful blue one!"

Mizpah looked bewildered.

"But such a thing never happened. All our uncles were married before we were born."

"All the better, but do as I say. I'll come with you," her husband replied.

Apparently strolling casually they went in search of Zara, and when they found her, Mizpah started to talk about their childhood.

"Forgive me, sister," Zara said, a trifle impatiently, "but I have much to do."

"Let me help you," Mizpah offered. "All this reminds me of when our uncle married. Don't you remember the fuss and excitement then. I was thinking of it this morning, and of the new robes we had. Mine was red, and yours was blue."

"Yes, of course," the false Zara replied quickly.

"You remember?" Mizpah asked.

"Why? Of course I do," was the reply.

Mizpah swayed and looked at her husband out of terrified eyes.

"That is very surprising," the husband said. "For you see no such thing ever happened. I set a trap for you, and you have fallen into it. You are not my wife's sister. Who are you?"

At this the impostor protested violently, but it was evident that she was very frightened. The Prince became more and more angry, and in the end the wretched girl threw herself on the ground and admitted the truth. When the Prince heard who her accomplices were he ordered their arrest at once, and by evening the tailor, his brother, and the girl, were locked up.

The real Zara and her friends waited in great anxiety until Mizpah sent a messenger for them, and then the sisters threw themselves into each other's arms.

When the bridegroom arrived next day there was no wedding but instead there was a feast, and the young man was most favourably impressed with the real Zara as she was with him.

Zara was amazed to find that she too, was now beautiful, in fact she was strikingly like Mizpah.

"Oh, how was it possible that I was so blind?" Mizpah exclaimed. "My own sister practically under my nose and I didn't recognise her, while that lying impostor managed to convince me."

All of which proves how little people sometimes see of what really goes on around them, and how easy it is to be deceived.

THE PIPING BIRD

SMALL BIRDS, LIKE small people, are often very ambitious. Sometimes they get ahead through merit, sometimes through cunning. Once there was a small bird who was determined that he was going to make an impression by fair means or foul. He had a thin, piping voice, and he desired above all things to be able to pipe up loudly, but no matter how hard he practised he was unable to make his little voice any bigger.

"If only I could get hold of a pipe of some kind, I could play," he told himself, and proceeded to hunt all through the forest to find something to make himself a pipe. But he found nothing. Then he worked out a very cunning scheme. Next door to him lived a fine large bird, who was inclined to treat the little bird with a good deal of contempt.

One day the little bird called on the large bird, and started what appeared to be a casual discussion.

"I hear that worms are likely to be short this season," he reported.

"Indeed," replied the large bird. "Well I don't worry, I can fly for miles if necessary, I expect I'll find enough!"

"I doubt it," the small bird replied. "I'm not worrying, of course, because I can go without food."

"How do you mean you can go without food?" the large bird asked.

"I've been training myself. Sometimes I don't eat for days and days on end. I believe I could fast for a week without minding very much."

"Ho," scoffed the large bird. "Well, if you could fast for a week I'm sure I could fast for two weeks."

26

"I don't believe anyone could do that!" exclaimed the small bird.

"If you could fast for one week, I could fast for two," asserted the large bird.

"Are you willing to bet on that?" the small bird asked.

"Of course I am. You'll have to supply me with two dozen large worms when I've won," chortled the large bird.

"I'll take you on. I'm quite sure you'll never last for two weeks without food."

"Oh, you'll see. Now, how are we going to do it?"

"Well, the only fair way is to seal ourselves up in our nests. As I'm the smallest I'd better do it. First of all I'll do the preliminary work. I'll seal you up, all except a small hole for your eye. Then you'll be able to watch me seal myself up, and see that there is no cheating. Then you can put the last bit in, in front of your eyes."

The large bird agreed enthusiastically. He was a very bumptious fellow, and was quite convinced that he could do anything twice as well as anyone else. So he sat complacently in his nest while the small bird built a wall all round him. Finally he was walled-in all but a small bit so that he could watch the other bird.

Then the small bird proceeded to build himself in until he was quite invisible. Then the large bird pulled the last bit of plaster in front of his own eyes, and proceeded to settle down and fast.

Now the cunning small bird, who was able to squeeze through the smallest possible space, had really left a slit through which he could fly in and out, and obtain food, but the foolish large bird was quite unaware of this. So the small bird woke up early, slipped out, and found some food and was back again by the time the sun rose. Not that either of them could see it rise, but they did feel its warmth.

"How are you?" called the small bird.

"I'm fine," replied the large one. "I don't mind being hungry in the least. How are you?"

"Oh, I'm fine too," replied the small bird, but he was very careful not to sound too convincing.

The next day passed in the same way, although this time the big bird's assertion that he was feeling "fine" sounded a little grim. On the third day the small bird felt sure that his fellow martyr's voice sounded faint, next day it was definitely faint, and on the day after that the small bird had to call twice before he got a reply. On the day after that there was no answer to his call. Nevertheless the small bird continued to apparently remain buried, and slipped out at night for food. When three more days had passed without any answer from the big bird, the small bird went across and opened the other nest. Inside the big bird was lying there, a mere skeleton.

"Dead for days past," commented the small bird. "Foolish, boasting fellow."

Then the small bird picked up the thigh bone of the big bird, put it to his beak and blew. A beautiful, mellow sound came forth. "Ha," exclaimed the small bird, "Now I shall be able to pipe with the best of them."

And pipe he did, flying round all day long, making a terrific din. This caused great excitement in the forest, for the small bird was so small, and so thin, with two legs like sticks, that the noise he made was most surprising. Not even a canary could have sung louder. After a time his noise caused a good deal of irritation, and a large canary determined to put a stop to it.

"Give me that pipe of yours?" he demanded.

The small bird puffed up all his feathers in great indignation.

"I will not. I had to go to great lengths to find this pipe, and I'm not giving it up."

"I don't believe you came by it honestly," retorted the canary, "but I don't care about that. Give it to me at once, or it will be the worse for you."

Quite unable to stand up against the canary the small bird was forced to hand over his pipe, and he flew away swearing vengeance on the canary.

The canary flew off home with the pipe, and showed it to his wife.

"I want you to look after this," he told her. "It belongs to that nasty little fellow who has been making such a din during the last few days. He's not to have it back on any account. So if anyone comes round trying to get it, just you be on your guard."

"But how shall I know him if he comes round?" asked Mrs. Canary.

"He's small, and he's got the thinnest little legs you ever saw, like sticks."

"All right," said Mrs. Canary. "I'll look out for those legs."

Sure enough while she was having a rest in her nest next day the thin little bird came around.

"I have called for my pipe," he told her. "I lent it to your husband yesterday, and told him I'd call for it this afternoon."

"Did you indeed? It's odd he didn't say so," replied Mrs. Canary.

"Oh, I expect he forgot," said the small bird. "Anyhow it doesn't matter. I'll take the pipe now."

"Indeed you won't," Mrs. Canary snapped at him. "I've heard all about you from my husband, and what a nuisance you have been making of yourself."

"But there must be some mistake, I have been doing nothing of the kind. You must be confusing me with someone else!"

"Oh, no, I'm not. You're the little bird with the thin legs, I'd know you anywhere. Fly off now, for you won't get the pipe!"

Furiously angry the small bird flew away, and then sat down to think out some way of getting back his pipe. He had no friends who would do it for him, because no one liked him very much, so he decided that he would disguise his legs. So he went round, and gathered up a lot of very tiny feathers, and stuck them all over his thin legs, then he added a few to his face as well, and back he went to the canary's nest. Having scouted round carefully he saw that Mrs. Canary was alone, so he flew up boldly.

"Good afternoon," he said in as deep a voice as he could manage. "Your husband asked me to collect that pipe you are minding."

Mrs. Canary peered at him suspiciously, first at his face, and then at his legs, but when she saw that he appeared to have thick, fat legs, she relaxed.

"He didn't say anything to me about your calling for the pipe," she protested weakly.

"I know, I only met him a while ago, and he told me about the annoyance that noisy little bird had caused playing on his pipe, so we decided the best thing was to bury the pipe, and save further trouble."

"Well, I think that's a very good idea," said Mrs. Canary. "It will save me the bother of looking after it all the time," and she gave him the pipe without demur.

A few minutes later her husband returned.

"I gave your friend the pipe," she told him. "Have you buried it safely?"

"What on earth are you talking about?" demanded the canary. She told him about the visitor.

"Good heavens," he yelled. "I didn't send anyone. It must have been that impudent little bird. Didn't I tell you to be cautious!"

"But I was," wailed his wife. "I looked at his legs most particularly, and they weren't thin at all. In fact they were fat and all covered with feathers."

"You're a very silly woman," exclaimed the canary, and immediately a quarrel flared up, and they had a most terrible row.

While they shrieked and flew at each other, they heard the pipe playing loudly above their heads, as the cunning little bird flew on his way, piping loudly.

Which only goes to show that you shouldn't judge by appearances.

WHY SHEEP SAY "MAA-A"

ONCE UPON A time there was a farmer with a son and daughter. The girl was gentle and quiet, and kept house for her father while he tended his farm. The boy caused his father a good deal of worry, however, for he didn't want to do any of the things ordinary people did. He was a clever fellow, and knew it, clever both with hands and tongue. There were only two things he really liked to do, one was to trap animals, the other was to make up songs, usually songs that gave him an opportunity to exercise his wit against his neighbours.

The father did not like the boy trapping animals, and forbade him to go into the forest, but the boy kept on begging to become a trapper. One day when the sister was going into the forest to gather sticks, the boy asked if he might go also. He asked for the loan of a machete so that he could cut branches to make traps. The father forbade the boy to trap but said he could go to the forest and help his sister gather sticks, and so make himself useful for once.

As soon as they were in the forest the boy dropped behind his sister, and used the sticks he gathered to make a trap. Then he lay down some distance away and watched. Very quickly his patience was rewarded, a hedgehog sniffed curiously round the trap, and was caught. In triumph the boy brought it home, set about making up the fire, and put the hedgehog to roast. Neither father nor sister had returned, so the son slipped back to the forest to set a few more traps.

When the father came home the first thing he noticed was a delicious smell, and then he saw the hedgehog roasting. At first he was angry because he knew the boy had been setting traps again, but after a while he wondered if he had been unjust. If the boy really wanted to become a trapper, perhaps he should be allowed

32

to do so. After all, it would provide them with good nourishing food. The father grew impatient waiting, the hedgehog was cooked, and he took it down and prepared to eat some of it. Just then the son returned and seeing what his father was doing, began to sing mockingly. He sang of how he had wanted to be a trapper, and how his father had forbade him, and refused to lend him a machete, and how he had managed to make a trap without it, and caught a hedgehog, and how he came home to find the father, who had refused to let him have his way, preparing to eat the hedgehog.

At this the poor father became very embarrassed, protesting that if the boy was set on trapping he would no longer forbid it, but that he would eat no more, neither of the hedgehog or anything else that might be caught. So he handed over the hedgehog to the son, only asking that a portion be saved for the sister who worked so hard. At that moment the girl returned with the sticks, and the son sang a song about how good she was, and how hard she worked, and how he would like to give her half the hedgehog to eat. She was hungry and gladly accepted, and they ate until they came to the last mouthful. The sister then said the brother must eat this, as he had caught the hedgehog, but the brother protested at great length, saying that she was entitled to it after all her hard work. So, after being pressed, the sister ate the last piece. No sooner had she done so, however, than the boy began to sing mockingly, telling the whole story over again from the very beginning, and adding that even the last bit of the hedgehog had not been given to him.

At this the sister became much upset, and felt very guilty. To make up for what she considered her greed, she offered her brother a very fine, long forked stick, which she had dragged from the forest. It was a shape much in demand at that time of the year, because it was possible to bend the branches of the pear trees with it, without damaging them, and to pluck the pears.

Very pleased with his own cleverness, the boy took the stick and marched off down the road. After he had gone some distance he saw a man picking his pear crop without a proper stick, and making a very bad job of it. So the boy pointed out to the man that he needed a proper stick. The man said he was sorry but he hadn't got a suitable stick, and as he was lame he couldn't go into the forest to get one. To this the boy replied that he had just the right stick, and he would loan it to the man. The man accepted the offer gratefully, used the stick to bend the branches, and gathered in a lot of pears, when unfortunately the stick broke. As soon as this happened the boy set up a great wail, and began to sing his song from the very beginning, with a new verse added about the man who had so carelessly broken his stick.

Naturally the man became chagrined. He explained that it was a sad mischance that he had broken the stick, as he was usually very skilful with such things, and offered the boy half of the pears to make up for it.

Delighted with his reward the boy gathered up the pears, and went on his way.

After a while he came to the blacksmith's forge. The blacksmith had just finished work, and a great fire was still glowing. The boy went up to the blacksmith and remarked what a shame it was to waste such a beautiful fire, and that it would be ideal for roasting pears (pears in West Africa are not like ours, and can only be eaten after they have been roasted). The blacksmith agreed but said he had no pears. At this the boy opened his bundle and displayed the fruit, saying the blacksmith could have all he wanted to eat if they could be roasted over his fire. The blacksmith was very pleased, so they set about roasting and eating the pears, and went on until they came to the last one. Then they had the usual polite argument until the boy convinced the blacksmith that he should have it. As soon as the blacksmith ate it, of course, the boy raised his voice in song, and went over every bit of the story, ending up with a new verse about how the blacksmith had eaten the last pear.

The blacksmith then became so convinced he had behaved like a churl that he begged the boy to take a very fine knife for tapping palm wine. The knife was worth far more than the pears, so the boy graciously accepted it, and walked off well satisfied with himself.

Down the road he saw a man tapping palm wine with a blunt knife, and damaging his trees, so the boy went up to him, and protested. "Look at the way you are destroying your trees with that blunt knife. Why don't you use a proper knife?" "I'm a poor man," replied the other, "and I have no money for a new knife."

"But I have a splendid one which I shall be pleased to lend you," said the boy, and handed it over. The man was delighted, and went on tapping with such speed that he soon had two large gourds of wine. Then to his horror the knife slipped, and snapped in two. Immediately the boy raised his voice, sang his song from the beginning, and added a new verse about the broken knife. This humiliated the man so much that he hastily offered half the palm wine, which was, of course, worth more than the knife. So the boy took up the gourd, and off he went.

A little further on he met an old woman. She looked tired and thirsty, so he stopped and offered her a drink of palm wine. The old woman was very glad, and between them they almost finished the wine. Then the boy insisted that the old woman must have the last drop. After a great deal of protest she took it, and was terribly overcome when the boy set up his song, and added a new verse about how she drank the last of his palm wine. Almost weeping with shame she sought for something to give him in exchange. "The thing I value most is a very fine razor," she told him. "You must have that." Now a razor, which is known as a "Maa" in the country we are concerned with here, is a very much valued object, and the boy was only too delighted with the exchange. He took it cheerfully and strode down the road feeling very elated at his own cleverness.

Next he came upon a shepherd leading a flock of sheep to a show. At once the boy noticed that the leading sheep had no bell, or other ornament to distinguish it. He pointed this out to the shepherd. "I know," the shepherd replied, "but the bell got broken, and I have no other." "Well," said the boy, "I haven't got a bell, but I can lend you this maa. It will at least glitter in the sun, and distinguish your leader." At first the shepherd protested, but the boy over-ruled his protests and forced the razor on him, and the shepherd tied it round the neck of the leading sheep. On they went, but when they arrived at the show, the maa was lost, and could not be found.

Again the boy set up his mocking song, this time with additions about the shepherd's carelessness and ingratitude. By this time the song was very long, and everybody, including the sheep, became very tired of listening, particularly as the boy made up not one, but several verses about the lost maa.

At last the sheep became so bored that the leader tried to drown the boy's voice by calling back "Maa-a," and all the other sheep took up the call, and went on "Maa-ing" until everyone was nearly deafened, and the boy turned tail and fled.

The story of his tricks spread, and people called "Maa-a" mockingly wherever he appeared. Worse still, sheep always called "Maa-a" too, and there were so many sheep everywhere in the district that the boy never had a chance to forget his cheap trickery. Finally, he left the place altogether, and went away to a district where there were no sheep, but he never made mocking songs against his neighbours again.

But because of the song about the razor, sheep all over the world always cry "Maa-a" ever since.

SING, CRICKET, SING

IT IS THE custom in West Africa to have a great ceremony when the head of a family dies. Everyone tries to contribute something, there is music, and people sing sad songs, and make up stories about the excellence of the person who has died. Relatives come from far and wide to attend the funeral.

When the mother-in-law of a farmer named Shan died, Shan felt that it was up to him to make a really impressive contribution to the mourning ceremony. The usual thing was to hire some professional mourners who would sing and wail for all they were worth. If they could sing louder, and wail more bitterly than anyone else present, all the better. Shan however was rather mean about money. He didn't like the idea of spending any, so he decided to do all the ceremonial mourning himself. Unfortunately he could neither play nor sing. However he collected a stringed instrument, and set out.

On the way through the forest he was surprised to hear what sounded like loud, and persistent scrapings of strings. "Ha, someone on the way to the funeral," he told himself. "Hi, there!" he called. Immediately there was complete silence. "That's odd," Shan thought, and stood still. After a moment or two the noise started up again, louder than ever. This time Shan didn't call, instead he moved very quietly towards the sound.

He soon found out the source of the noise. Two large crickets were sitting on a log, chirruping away, and making a terrible din. Closer and closer crept Shan, but the crickets were so busy they

37

didn't hear him, and knew nothing of his presence until he clapped a bag down on them, and imprisoned them.

"Listen," Shan told them. "I'm not going to hurt you. Quite the contrary, I'm going to do you a good turn. I'm going to take you with me to a distant village, and when we get there, wait for the word from me, and then sing. Keep on singing until I tell you to stop, and I'll reward you well."

Naturally the crickets were a bit flurried and indignant at the way he had pounced on them, but as they were his prisoners anyhow, it seemed best to agree to his proposal.

"Very well, but you might have asked us first," said the youngest cricket. "And mind you keep your word, and reward us!" chimed in the elder.

"I'll reward you," Shan assured them. "Now keep very quiet until I tell you to sing."

When Shan arrived at the village people gathered round, and asked where his mourners were. To this Shan replied that this was no ordinary occasion, and he wasn't going to take the easy way out. He was going to do his own mourning, and he would play for them. This made a great impression, and everyone sat down and waited for Shan to make music. So Shan sat and prepared to twang the stringed instrument he had brought.

"Sing now," he whispered to the crickets, and the crickets started off in an amazing rhythm. On and on went the noise, and everyone marvelled at this tireless performance, for the longer a mourner could go on the higher the esteem in which he was held.

At last when even the crickets were feeling a bit worn out Shan hissed, "Stop," and laid down his instrument. Everyone crowded round and congratulated him, and invited him to come to the feast. At this the crickets leapt inside the bag. Pressing them down with his hand, Shan shook his head.

"I can only eat if I am left alone. I feel this is too sad an occasion to mingle with others, even my dearest friends. If you will give me a share of food and close the door behind I shall eat!"

Much awed, the people did this, and when he was safely alone Shan brought out the crickets.

"See now, how I keep my word. You can share this feast with me," he said. The crickets danced for joy and jumped on the table.

"One moment," Shan said quickly. "Before you eat, you must wash your hands." The crickets apologised for their breach of etiquette and got down off the table. "There is a bowl of water,"

Shan told them. So the crickets walked over to the bowl and washed their hands. Then they walked back again. Now as they walked on both fore legs and hind legs, naturally when they walked across the floor and climbed on the table they were as dirty as ever.

When Shan saw this he set up a loud cry, and commanded the crickets to go wash and wash once more, while he began to eat. This the poor crickets proceeded to do, but of course no matter how carefully they walked, each time they got back to the table they were far from clean, and they were still going back and forth and becoming more and more hungry when there was a knocking on the door, and a voice asked Shan if he was coming to play again.

At this Shan seized the crickets and thrust them back into the bag. "Have patience," he commanded, "I'll arrange things better next time." Before he left he put all the food he couldn't eat into another bag he was carrying. Then he went out, and started his performance again, and the crickets had to sing all night long without any food.

It was nearly morning when all was over, and by that time the crickets were quite exhausted. Everyone pressed round Shan and told him what a wonderful musician he was, and begged him to remain another day and play again, but Shan refused, saying he was really too sad to play any more. At dawn he went on his way.

After he had walked for an hour or so the sun began to get hot so Shan lay down and went to sleep. While he was asleep, the angry crickets managed, by making the most tremendous efforts, to escape from the bag. Then they crept into the other bag where the food was and demolished every crumb. After that they hurried away as fast as they could.

Shan woke up feeling very pleased with himself. He had been the hero of the ceremony, it had not cost him anything, and he had some very nice leftovers for his breakfast. He decided that he would even share with the crickets, so he opened the bag, and told them they might come out. When nothing happened he shook the bag gently, thinking that they were still asleep. When this did no good he turned it upside down, and then it dawned on him that the crickets had escaped.

"Oh well, all the more breakfast for me," he said cheerfully, and picked up the food bag. He didn't need to open that to know it was empty. Realising what had happened he howled with rage, and called the crickets thieves and villains. He made so much noise that all the animals, birds and insects round about stopped to listen.

"Gather round, everyone," called Shan. "Come and hear what those low, dishonest crickets have done to me. I allowed them to sing so that they might earn some food. Now they have stolen all the food while I slept, and made off. Go, and find them, and bring them here. Until justice is done, all crickets will share in the disgrace!"

Now crickets are clever little fellows, and they decided that there were probably two sides to the story, so sitting well out of reach they proceeded to question Shan as to what had happened.

Somehow his answers did not satisfy them, and they soon guessed that somehow Shan had tried to cheat the crickets, and they had got the better of him.

"Wait until dusk, and then we shall find them," a wise old cricket told Shan. "In the meanwhile you go home, and wait."

Unwillingly Shan went, and as he walked he planned all kinds of ways in which he would have revenge on the crickets.

At dusk the crickets set out to look for their brethren, but as they went they sang loudly so that no one could fail to hear their approach, so of course the culprits were never found. Next morning they reported their failure to Shan who was highly indignant, and ordered them to go out again that evening or he would take revenge on the whole tribe of crickets.

Next morning the crickets returned to report failure once more, and so it went on until Shan became an old man, and died himself. But the crickets still go out at dusk and sing a song of warning to the two thieves who stole Shan's food. If you go out on a fine warm evening, and sit in a wood or a field you will hear them, just like little fiddlers playing on a stringed instrument.

THE FISHERMAN

In some parts of Africa people earn a living by fishing in the deep rivers. Once there were two brothers who left their home in the forest and journeyed until they came to a place where there was a great deal of fishing. Deciding they would like this life they settled down, and learned how to catch fish. Later on they became friendly with an old man and his daughter who lived nearby. This girl was handsome, and a very hard worker, and after a time both brothers fell in love with her, and the girl couldn't decide which of them she would marry.

"Marry the one who is the best fisherman," her grandmother advised her. "Both the young men are strangers, and we know very little about them. See which one catches the most fish within the next few weeks. Let each one go off and fish alone, without help from anyone else, and we'll soon see who is the best man!"

The girl thought this over, and decided that at any rate the plan would give her time to decide which young man she liked best. They were both handsome, both quite clever, and there seemed little to choose between them. So she told her father what her grandmother had suggested, and he told the young men that his daughter would marry the best fisherman.

The elder of the young men was known as Suki and the younger as Kana. They decided that the girl's decision was fair enough, and that they would do their best to catch as many fish as possible. So next morning they went their separate ways. Soon after mid-day Kana returned with a fine catch of fish. "Have you done fishing for the day?" asked the grandmother. "Yes," replied Kana. "Then perhaps you will chop some wood for me?" "Certainly, I will try and find time," said Kana, and off he went to

41

chop wood, and after that he did several other jobs, when the worst of the heat was over.

It was evening when Suki returned, looking extremely tired, but carrying quite a good load of fish.

"You put in a long day," remarked the girl's father. "That is the way I work," Suki replied.

One day passed after another, and each time Kana returned early with a load of fish, and Suki returned late with another load of fish. Suki was always tired out after his long day's labour, and Kana seemed quite fresh and cheerful.

"Well, it's easy to see who is the best worker," remarked the father. "Kana only gives a few hours to the job, he must be like the butterfly who can't stay in one spot for any length of time. Suki is the real worker."

"But look how much help Kana gives to others," the girl pointed out, "Suki only does his fishing!"

"That's as it should be," the father assured her. "Suki is a good steady worker."

"But he doesn't catch any more fish than Kana," the girl protested.

"The poor fellow has bad luck. I think he's too anxious, and scares the fishes. When you marry him you will find he'll catch twice as many," said the father.

By this time the girl, who had seen a good deal more of Kana than she had of Suki, felt sure it was Kana she would prefer to marry and she was very worried because Kana seemed lazy and flighty in comparison with his brother. So one day when Kana came home early as usual she decided to talk to him about it.

"You know," she said. "I expected that you would work very hard in order to marry me."

"I work as I've always worked," replied Kana. "Surely you would not wish me to deceive you by making false efforts?"

"Not exactly, but why do you not stay longer and bring back more fish?"

"I always bring back a full load, to bring any more would be wasteful," Kana told her.

This was reasonable, but the girl was not satisfied.

"My father thinks Suki is a far better worker than you are!" she remarked.

"And what do you think?" enquired Kana.

"I'm afraid it's the truth," she replied, and went away feeling sad.

Then Suki arrived, looking tired, and a bit forlorn, and everyone fussed round making him a meal, and seeing that he spent a restful evening, while Kana joined in the singing and dancing round the fire. This annoyed the father more than ever. "Well I'm glad I put those two young men to a test," he told his daughter. "It didn't take long to prove which one was best. When the crops are in you shall marry Suki!"

This made the girl very angry, because she felt that Kana was making little of her. If he seriously wanted to marry her surely he would work harder, and harder, to prove himself the best worker. She did not want to marry Suki.

"It's all very well for father," she told her grandmother, "but I don't think it's going to be much fun marrying a man who works from morning until night and comes home too tired to talk, or dance, or sing."

"Then you would really like to marry Kana?" asked the grandmother.

"Of course not," snapped the girl. "He is making me look ridiculous!"

The grandmother hid a smile and spoke no more of the matter. Next morning after the two men had gone fishing as usual, she made a suggestion.

"Why not visit Suki. It must be dull for him to be there, alone all day long. Take him some food, and that will give you an opportunity to know him better. I'd creep up, and give him a nice surprise. You may find him quite different to what you think!"

At first the girl was unwilling, but then she decided to go. By this time she was so tired of turning the problem over in her mind, that she felt it was better to do anything than nothing, so she wrapped up some food, and set off for the place where Suki fished.

It was very hot and unpleasant, and she was sorry she had set out on such an errand, but she continued on her way until she saw the river in the distance. Then she went very softly to the spot where she expected to find Suki.

She was surprised to see some nets lying on the ground, and then when she looked again she saw a figure sleeping under a tree. She was surprised but thought perhaps Suki was having a brief rest, so she lay down in the shade and rested too. Hours passed, sometimes Suki woke, yawned, stretched, looked at the sun and then went to sleep once more. Finally, when it was late afternoon he

rose, went to his nets, and fished. The girl rose to her feet without a word, and slipped away.

When she got home her grandmother was watching for her.

"Well, did you surprise Suki?" asked the grandmother.

"I didn't go near him after all, so please say nothing," replied the girl.

When Suki returned home a little later, he seemed, as usual, to be weary, and carried a small load of fish. Kana, who had been back for hours, and who had been doing various odd jobs, passed no comment.

"Have you had a hard day, Suki?" the girl enquired. Suki nodded.

"A fisherman's life is not easy. I have not got Kana's luck!"

"I wonder if it is luck?" the girl remarked, and walked away from him.

She felt very angry at the way Suki had deceived them all, and resolved to expose him for what he was, lazy and hypocritical. Next day she told her grandmother she would really visit Suki this time, so once more she packed food, and set off. Again she crept up to the fishing ground, and once more she saw Suki asleep under a tree while his nets lay idle. So she turned and went back to her grandmother, and told her the truth. "I want you and my father to come with me and see for yourselves; then this pretence will have to come to an end!"

When the father heard the story he was scarcely able to believe it, and insisted that there must be an explanation, but the girl reminded him that she had watched Suki for hours on the previous day and he had done no work.

"Perhaps he was feeling ill," suggested the father. "Then he ate a fine supper for a man who was feeling ill," snapped the daughter.

"I don't like spying on him, anyhow," the father complained.

"Nonsense, he's been deceiving us for weeks," retorted the daughter. "Come on!"

So she led them back through the bush, and finally they sighted the river. Then the girl made them go slowly, and carefully until they could peer through the bushes. There the same picture met their eyes that the girl had seen earlier. The nets were lying on the bank, and Suki was asleep.

"What did I tell you!" whispered the daughter.

"A man's entitled to a rest," protested the father.

"He's been resting since early morning, and he'll rest till late afternoon if you watch," said the girl. So she made the two others lie down, and wait. Every time they dozed off to sleep she wakened them again, and this didn't improve their tempers, but she was determined that they would see how Suki cheated.

After several hours Suki roused himself, looked at the sun, then got to work, and gathered some fish in his net. Finding his load a bit heavy he threw some back in the river, and then he set off for the village at a slow pace. By hurrying along by-paths the trio got home before him, and were tending the fire when he arrived, and threw himself down wearily.

"Suki, would you fetch some wood for the fire?" asked the grandmother.

Suki sighed.

"I've had a very hard day, can't Kana get it?"

"Here it is," said Kana, and threw a bundle on the ground.

After supper was over the girl's father said he had something to say.

"You two young men have now been fishing for some weeks, and I feel the time has come to give my consent to a marriage with my daughter!"

Suki smiled and looked at Kana triumphantly, but he pretended to be modest.

"I'm afraid you may find the decision a difficult one. I know my brother does not stick to his job as he should, but he is quick and clever. On the other hand, I don't profess to be the clever one, I just like to work away and keep on till the job is done."

"Cheat!" cried the girl in anger.

Suki looked amazed.

"What does this mean?" he asked.

"It means I didn't want to marry you anyhow," cried the girl, "but after what I have seen yesterday and today, I know you are not only lazy but a cheat as well. You see I went to visit you yesterday!"

"To give you a little surprise," said the grandmother slyly.

"I was the one who got the surprise," went on the girl, "for I saw that you slept nearly all day, and only worked for an hour or so. Then you came back here pretending to be tired."

"How can you say such a thing," exclaimed Suki. "It would be terrible if your father and grandmother believed this story."

"We saw for ourselves," put in the grandmother. "You see we all went to visit you again this day!"

Suki was very indignant at this, and protested his innocence, but it was no use. The father agreed with his daughter that Kana was the proper man to be her husband, and arrangements were made for the wedding. Everyone was so angry with Suki that he had to leave the village, and go down to the coast where he had to work much harder at fishing in order to earn a living.

So the next time you meet someone who always seems to be very busy, and who never has time to help anyone else, remember Suki and the fish. It isn't always the busy people who work the hardest.

HOW THE DOGS CAME

A LONG TIME ago there were no domestic animals, all were wild, and all were the enemy of man. They feared him, and he feared them, unless they were too small to do him any harm. There were no dogs such as we know today, but creatures roamed the forest who were a mixture of wolf, hyena and jackal. These creatures were not friendly with any of the animals. They killed smaller, weaker beasts for food, and they ran and hid when large animals appeared. If an animal was wounded or dying, they attacked and ate him.

Sometimes when they roamed around, they watched man curiously. They saw that man had shelter and warmth, and that he hunted for his food, and didn't hunt alone, but in groups. They both despised and envied him.

Now it came to pass that there was a great drought, and food was scarce, and the wild dogs had to hunt harder than they had ever hunted before. One day a mother left her litter while she sought for food. It so happened that a number of families were moving to a new district because of the drought, as people often do in Africa, for one reason or another. They were resting from the heat of the day, and a very small boy wandered off by himself and came across the litter of puppies. They were very tiny, and the small boy was curious. He picked up one of the puppies, and decided he would keep it. So he wrapped it up in a bundle, and took it away. He was very anxious to own this strange little creature, but he was afraid his mother would not allow it, so he hid

48

the puppy, and no one knew he had it until that night when they had gone much further on their journey. At supper time the little boy gave the puppy some of his own supper, and then the mother discovered the animal.

"What are you doing with that?" she asked. "You don't have to hunt for your own food yet."

"It's not for food," said the little boy. "I want it to keep."

"But who wants to keep an animal?" the mother asked. "You'll have to feed it and food is scarce."

"I know," said the boy. "But I'll give it some of mine. I have no brothers or sisters to share with."

Because the mother was fond of the child she argued no more, but let him keep the puppy. The puppy was very happy, because he had more food and was more comfortable than he had ever been before. He shared the boy's meals, and slept beside him at night.

In the meanwhile the mother dog missed the puppy, and was very angry. Man was her enemy, and she could smell his scent round the litter, and she was sure her child had been taken away, and eaten, so she resolved to have her revenge, and set off to trail the robber.

She travelled for a long time before she caught up with the people, who had now settled in a new spot. She came to their village one afternoon when everyone was resting, and was amazed to see her son asleep under a tree in the arms of a child. She was about to attack the child when fortunately her son smelled her scent, and came gambolling over to her. With a soft snarl the mother picked him up by the scruff of the neck, and dragged him into the bush, where she set him down.

"At last I have found you, and rescued you, my poor child," she panted.

"You haven't rescued me," yapped the puppy. "I was very well looked after, and I was having a fine time. I live as well as man, and he lives much better than we do."

"My poor, foolish child," said the mother, "don't you know that man is our enemy."

"I don't believe it," said the puppy. "Everyone was very kind to me."

"Be sensible," snapped the mother. "They were only fattening you up so they could kill, and eat you."

"I don't believe it," said the puppy. "The child loved me."

"You don't know what you are talking about," said the mother. "I am very displeased with you. Come along home now, and don't think of these foolish notions any more."

The puppy opened his mouth to protest, but she picked him up by the scruff of the neck again, which made it impossible for him to talk, and off she loped back to the litter.

Days passed but the puppy didn't feel happy. He missed the food, and he missed the little boy, and he was no longer a special person, he was just one of a litter, and he didn't like it. Days lengthened into weeks, and the puppy grew big, and strong, but still he didn't forget the happy time he had spent with man. So one night he slipped away again, set his nose to the trail, and started back in search of the village.

So eager was he to get there that he did something no wild animal ever does, but which dogs do to this day. He didn't stop for food, or drink, or rest, so early next morning he arrived at the village, tired, and thirsty and hungry.

The little boy who had missed the puppy very much was playing by himself outside his house. Suddenly he heard yells from the people around, and looked up to see an animal streaking towards him. "Run, run, you'll be killed," shouted the villagers, but the next moment the animal had reached the little boy, and instead of attacking him, it jumped up, and licked him, wagging its tail frantically.

"It's my pup," shrieked the little boy. "He's come back!" and he threw his arms round the creature's neck, and hugged it. The villagers were amazed at this, for they were afraid of the puppy now that it had grown, but the little boy gave the animal water and food and then they curled up together and went to sleep.

Back in the bush the mother dog missed her son, and decided to follow him, and this time she brought the rest of the litter with her because they were big enough to walk. So they all put their noses on the trail of their brother, and away they went. The mother was so angry and anxious to get her son back that they also went steadily on, pausing for nothing until they reached the edge of the village.

There they saw their brother playing with the little boy. The boy was throwing a stick, and the puppy was fetching it back to him to throw again, and they were both enjoying the game.

"Oh look at your poor, foolish brother," whined the mother. "Look at him playing tricks."

The pups all looked, and the eldest said, "I don't see that it's so foolish, I think it's fun."

"It won't be fun when he's killed and eaten," growled the mother.

Just then a man came in with a carcass which he proceeded to cut up, and as he cut he threw bits to the pup.

"Just look at that," said his brother watching enviously. "It doesn't look as if *he's* going to be killed, and eaten!"

"Don't be foolish," cried the mother. "Hasn't man always been our enemy."

"Well, he's not our brother's enemy," said the eldest pup. "I wish we were with him."

The mother was so annoyed she cuffed her son, and knocked him down.

"Don't contradict your mother," she snarled.

Just then the pup wandered away from the boy, and came towards his family. When he saw them he was delighted, and ran up to sniff them.

"Welcome, brothers," he yelped. "You must come, and meet my friends."

"Don't be ridiculous," cried the mother. "Your brothers are not going to be foolish like you. Come on home at once."

But the pup was too big to take orders now, and he refused.

"I'm not going," he told her. "Man is my friend, and I have a far better life than I had in the bush. I'm staying here."

At this the anxious mother broke into a wild protest.

"All right," she cried, "but don't dare to come back to us when man turns against you. Come, my children, let us go."

Now the others didn't want to go, but they were afraid, so they followed their mother, leaving the pup behind.

The pup trotted back, and started to play again. He was sorry to lose his family, but he felt he really belonged to the boy who had brought him up. So he stayed in the village, and grew bigger, and soon he began to go out hunting with the men, and the boy came along too. When the dog killed an animal or a bird he brought it to the boy, because he knew he'd get a share.

When the pup grew into a big dog he was out one day when he met a young wild dog, and stopped to talk to her. By this time a good many wild dogs knew about their extraordinary brother who lived with man, so the young dog began to question him about it.

He told her of his life, and suggested that she should come to the village and see for herself. Afraid, but greatly daring, she went there with him. She was too shy and frightened to be friendly at first, but the dog shared his food with her, and she soon came every day. In the end she became the wife of the dog, and when she had puppies of her own the dog brought the boy to see them.

As soon as the puppies could walk they staggered after their father into the village. At first the mother was frightened, and took them back, one by one, by the scruff of the neck, but as soon as they got free they toddled off to the village once more, until in the end she had to let them be, and came and lived there herself.

Now these puppies in turn grew up, and became attached to owners, and went hunting. Strangers passing through the village marvelled at this, and they too began to take wild puppies from litters and bring them into the villages.

Gradually the puppies who grew up with man began to change their dispositions as well as their habits. They were friendly with their owners, and not with others. They hunted wild animals, or chased them if they came near the villages. In fact they began to change into the kind of dogs we know today. If they got lost they became very unhappy until they found their owners again.

As time passed these tame dogs changed in appearance also, and no longer resembled jackals or hyenas.

Now every village, not only in Africa, but all over the world has its dogs.

But the wild dogs didn't change, they remained the same. They are surly, evil tempered creatures, who don't like other animals very much, and don't like each other either.

THE BOY AND THE GENII

THE FARMER HASSAN, had an only child who was a very spoiled boy. He was never willing to do what he was told. If anyone asked him to do anything, he always asked, "Why?" and if the reason given didn't satisfy him, he simply didn't do as he was asked. It was intelligent, of course, to want to know why things should be done, but it wasn't very clever to assume that other people didn't have very good reasons for what they did.

It was the custom in the village to stay at home on certain days, and to go and work on the farm land on others, leaving the village empty. One day when Hassan and his wife were going off to the farm, the boy said he didn't feel like going and he wanted to stay at home.

"But you can't stay in the village today," the father told him.

"Why not?" asked the boy. "What's different about today?"

"I don't want to go into that," said the father. "You will just have to take my word for it for once, and come along with us."

"If you stay here today there will be no proper food for you until we come home this evening," the mother pointed out.

"I don't care, any scraps will do for me," the boy replied. "But unless you can give me some very good reason for going to the farm today I shall stay at home."

The mother and father looked at each other anxiously. They didn't want to tell the boy that on certain days, and this was one of them, the genii visited the village, and spent the day there. They would tap the palm wine, and sing and dance, and do no real harm, but they would become annoyed if any human saw them. Parents never told their children about this because they were afraid that the little ones would become curious and creep back to watch the genii and get themselves into trouble.

"I want you to come to the farm with us today," the boy's father said seriously. "There is much work to be done!"

"I'll come tomorrow and work," the boy replied obstinately, for he sensed that there was some secret he didn't know. "But I'll stay at home today."

The father and mother looked at him helplessly.

"If you *will* stay at home, then I'll have to lock you in the house," the mother informed him. "The village will be deserted, anyone might come along, and you wouldn't be safe here alone."

"That's right," the father joined in. "We can't leave you to wander about alone. If you stay we'll have to lock you in, so I think you will agree that it would be a lot more pleasant to come to the farm with us."

Now the boy didn't like the idea of being left alone, it made him a little afraid, but by now he wouldn't give in, so he replied airily.

"Lock me up if you wish, but I'm not going to the farm today."

So the parents left scraps of food and a jar of water with him, and prepared to depart.

"Remember one thing," said his father, "if you hear any unusual noises just remain quiet. Don't call out."

The boy only smiled, and the parents went away in a very worried frame of mind. They would have preferred to stay with their foolish child, but they knew if they did that the genii might become spiteful, and do something to upset the whole village.

After they had gone the village became very quiet and lonely, and the boy regretted his decision. There was nothing he could do in the house, and after a while he lay down to pass the time in sleep.

He had been asleep a short time when he was awakened by the sound of singing, and laughing, although he did not recognise the voices. It was still far too early for the return of the villagers.

Then the boy heard footsteps, light footsteps, and then he heard some people swarming up the palm trees, and the "tap, tap, tap," of someone tapping the palm wine.

"Ho," he cried out. "Who is tapping the wine?"

Immediately there was dead silence followed by a confused outburst.

"Who called?" asked a voice, but the boy didn't reply. The strangers couldn't see him, and the boy thought he would have some fun with them.

"There can be no one here, it must have been some bird calling," another voice replied.

"I thought it sounded like a boy," someone else said.

"Nonsense, who would have the audacity to stay here on *our* day," the other voice replied, and after a second or two the tapping began again.

"Who taps the palm wine?" the boy sang again. Once more there was silence, and then a louder outburst.

"There is someone!"

"The impudence, let us search every house!"

Immediately there was a sound of many footsteps going in various directions, as doors were tried. The boy, now a little alarmed, remained quite still, telling himself that he was quite safe from the visitors, whoever they were, as the door was locked.

Finally someone tried the door.

"This door is locked," said a voice.

"Command it to open," said another.

"Open door," said the first voice, and to his amazement the boy saw the door open all by itself, and a little man came in. He was a very light brown, and he had queer, light eyes.

"So there you are, impudent one," he cried out when he saw the boy. "Come out here," and he dragged the boy out of the house.

The boy blinked in surprise. He found himself surrounded by a large crowd of little people whom he had never seen before, some dressed in the most remarkable, and colourful garments. One of them wore an enormous turban on his head and carried a tall stick.

"Come here," he commanded. Nervously the boy went forward.

"What do you mean by remaining in the village today? Are you ill?"

"No," the boy replied boldly. "But it's my home, and why should I leave it today?"

"Because on this day the village is ours, and you have no right to remain. Why were you allowed to remain?"

"I wasn't. I simply refused to go with my father, so he locked me up," the boy replied. "Who are you?"

"That's no business of yours, mind your manners," was the answer, and then another man stepped forward.

"Your Highness, this is a most impudent youth. He has broken the law, and he should be severely punished."

"He shall be punished," snapped the man in the turban. "Tie him up. I'll decide what to do with him later!"

Before the boy could protest he found himself tied to a tree. Then his captors seemed to forget all about him. They busied themselves collecting palm wine, which they proceeded to drink, and then they made merry, dancing, singing, and performing the most remarkable conjuring tricks the boy had ever seen. He was so enthralled that he forgot to be scared. It was all so fascinating that the boy didn't realise how much time had passed until he saw a man hurry to speak to the chief of these peculiar people.

"Highness," the man panted. "Two people approach the village, and it wants an hour to sunset. They are breaking the rules. Shall we capture them?"

The chief looked very annoyed.

"What is the world coming to; more people breaking the rules. Certainly capture them, and bring them to me."

The little man scurried away and a few minutes later the boy was horrified to see his father and mother being led in by a group of men who looked like soldiers. They cast his parents down on the ground before the chief.

"What do you mean by coming here? You know you are breaking the rules," the chief said angrily.

"Master," said the father. "We beg for mercy, we are the parents of this unhappy boy. We feared for his safety and came back early."

"You should never have left him here," the chief said coldly.

"We could not drag him by force, and he would not come of his own free will," the father cried.

"Then you have brought him up badly, and it is time he was taught a lesson in obedience. We shall take him with us, and he'll soon learn."

At this the boy's mother wailed loudly.

"Oh, no, Highness," she implored. "He is but a foolish child. Spare him to us, and I'm sure he will never disobey again."

"He won't have the chance," replied the chief. "He is coming to work in my service, and he'll learn to do as he's told."

"Highness, I can't let you take him," cried the father.

The chief seemed to swell with rage.

"What? You dare to oppose me? You know what it means?"

"I know what it means, Highness, but what does anything matter if I lose my only child," replied the father.

"Perhaps you would like to arrange a contest," said the chief. "Perhaps you would like to wrestle with my best wrestler with the boy as a prize for the winner."

"Oh, no, no," cried the mother. "Spare my husband!"

"If you won't give me a chance to get my boy back on any other terms, I'll accept the challenge," the father answered quietly.

At this everyone in the crowd began to comment, and laugh. It was clear that they regarded such a contest as a joke, and didn't believe that the boy's father would stand the slightest chance of winning against the wrestler.

"Come, wrestler," called the chief. "Here is some sport for you!"

The crowd parted and a small thickset man, with the most enormous muscles appeared. The boy's father tried to hide his despair. He had always been a very good wrestler, but he had never been up against anyone like the individual who now confronted him. The man looked as if his muscles were made of steel.

The crowd cleared a space, and with the chief sitting in the foreground, the wrestler and the boy's father circled round each other, while the mother wept, and the boy gave himself and his family into the care of the spirits, for he had no hope.

At first the wrestler seemed to throw the boy's father about like a sack of meal, but gradually the father, fighting with the courage of desperation, began to hold his own. Slowly and grimly the struggle went on. Both men were beginning to look distressed. Finally the wrestler seemed to gather himself together to make one supreme effort to finish the contest, but it failed, and while the watching crowd held its breath in amazement, the father got the wrestler off the ground, threw him with all his strength, and the creature fell, and remained still.

The chief stared in amazement.

"Well," he gasped. "That is the first time my wrestler has ever been beaten. How did you do it? Do you know some new tricks we haven't heard about?"

The father shook his head.

"No, Highness, it's just that I love my son."

The chief nodded his head.

"Then take him. But remember he must never break the rules again. And you, boy, remember that. Because if ever I catch you in further disobedience I'll take you to my country, and we'll teach you obedience there."

"Highness, I shall never again disobey," quavered the boy.

"Remember well," said the chief, and raised his stick.

There was a sound of great wings rushing through the air, and then the boy found himself alone with his parents. He rubbed his eyes in amazement. All the strange people had vanished in a second, including the wrestler.

"Where are they?" he gasped.

"Who?" the father asked.

"All the strange people!"

"You have been asleep," said the father.

"But I haven't," gasped the boy. "I was wide awake. I was tied up in ropes."

"Where are they?"

The boy looked down. He was sitting on the ground but there were no ropes.

"There were strange people here, they threatened me. I'll go and find them. I tell you they were here."

"You will come into the house," his father said.

"But," the boy protested, and then he stopped. He remembered what the strange chief had said about disobedience. "Very well, I'll come into the house," he finished weakly.

"That's right," his mother told him. "Do as your father says."

"I had a dream—a very queer dream," the boy said questioningly. His father looked at him but didn't answer. They never spoke of the matter again. The boy was afraid to ask questions, and his father and mother behaved as if nothing had happened.

As the days passed the boy decided that it had all been a dream, but nevertheless he took no chances, and from that time onwards he was obedient, even if he didn't always understand the reasons for everything his father asked of him.

HOW ENEMIES ARE MADE

ONE OF THE most terrible things that can happen in the bush is a fire, because there is no way of putting it out. Everything is destroyed and animals who cannot flee swiftly and escape, are overcome by smoke and burnt or suffocated.

One day a very severe fire swept over the bush, and all the animals fled towards the river bank. Most of them could swim, and they reached the other side in safety. Those who could not swim, such as the monkeys, clung on to the larger animals, and were carried across. Like the monkeys, the hare was unable to swim, but unlike the monkeys, who were at least tolerated by everyone, nobody wanted to carry the hare across because he was a very cunning fellow, and had got the better of several simple people.

So now he ran wildly up and down the bank of the river, imploring various animals to take him across. First he asked the lion, who roared, "Out of my way!" and dashed past him into the water. Then he tried an elephant, but the elephant had a load of monkeys clinging to him, and he shook his trunk and walked on. Next the hare approached a leopard, but the leopard snarled, and jumped into the stream. Lastly the hare approached a wild dog, but the dog had once been tricked by the hare so he now ignored him.

Finally the hare saw that a small boat was anchored near the river bank. His only hope of being saved was that someone fleeing from the fire would escape by boat, so he crept under a bundle of mats that were lying at the bottom of the boat, and lay still while the fire crept nearer, and nearer, and the hare could hear the crackling of the flames. Just as he had given himself up for lost he heard running footsteps, and a man and his wife dashed out from among the trees and made for the boat. They leapt in, and a moment later were paddling wildly for the opposite shore. The hare breathed a huge sigh of relief, and as soon as the boat reached the bank he leapt out and ran off.

However, he was not a fellow to forget an injury, and he had sworn to have revenge on the people who would not carry him across the river. So he set out to find the lion. He found him at last, settled down in a cave, but not enjoying himself very much in his new home.

"I am indeed glad to see that you escaped safely from the fire!" the hare told him. "Thanks," growled the lion, feeling a little embarrassed that the hare should refer to the matter.

"I got away very comfortably," the hare went on. "A kind man rowed me over. Of course, it's hard to settle down in a new place, but what can one do. Even if the fire hadn't burnt one's old home, thieves would have taken everything."

"I'd like to see a thief take anything of mine," roared the lion.

"Oh, but one did, didn't you know?" said the hare with an air of surprise.

"What do you mean?" growled the lion.

"Why I passed your old cave after you had left on the day of the fire, I saw the elephant absolutely wrecking the place," said the hare.

The lion shook the ground under them with his roaring.

"Well, I'm sorry to have upset you like this, I'm sure," remarked the hare. "I shouldn't think any more about it if I were you. There is nothing you can do anyhow!"

"Ho, isn't there," said the lion savagely, and sat down to brood, while the hare well pleased with himself, went off.

Next he sought the elephant, whom he found under a huge, shady tree. "Oh, so you haven't moved!" commented the hare.

"What do you mean, moved?" asked the elephant. "I've only been here a few days since the fire."

"I know," the hare replied, "but I heard the leopard say that it was unfair that you should have this tree to sleep under as it's exactly what he needs, but that if he tries to sleep over your head your snores would keep him awake. I understood he was going to demand that you leave."

"Indeed," trumpeted the elephant, "what impertinence. I certainly shall not leave!"

Then the hare sought out the leopard.

"I'm afraid you are having a pretty thin time here," he remarked.

"Well, the hunting isn't too good," agreed the leopard, "but I expect it's because the place is new to me. When I get to know it better I'll be all right."

"I'm afraid not," the hare said with apparent sympathy. "You see the wild dog is determined to starve you out, and have the place to himself, and he's scaring off all the animals he doesn't catch for himself. I saw him chasing a herd of deer only this morning."

At this the hungry leopard became furious.

"I'll teach him," he snarled. "Just you wait and see what I'll do to him!"

Later in the day there were terrible fights. The lion sought out the elephant, and attacked him, and the elephant practically strangled the lion, and then went in search of the leopard and almost strangled him too. The leopard only escaped by running away, but happening to encounter the wild dog he flew at him and almost killed him.

From that day to this, and all because of the hare's mischief making, none of these animals are friendly. Elephants always know when there is a lion in the vicinity, and become very uneasy. Leopards will attack elephants, or for that matter almost any other beast. The wild dog seems to fear attack from almost any animal bigger than himself, and trusts nobody. The hare, who is the only one who knows the truth of the matter, still pretends to be everybody's friend.

THE TORTOISE AND HIS MOTHER

MONKEYS ARE CLEVER people, and when they are greedy as well, they may cause a great deal of trouble. Chita was greedy, and when he had nothing else to do, he used to sit around and plot and plan about all sorts of things, but mainly he concerned himself with schemes to get hold of more food. One day Chita conceived a brilliant idea. There was just so much food in the forest, usually enough for everyone, sometimes insufficient just before the rains came, but Chita would have liked a lot more. "If a whole lot of people could be persuaded to go away, or even if they could be forced to go away, all the food would be left for the others," Chita whispered to himself.

The problem was, who would go away? At first Chita thought he would start a campaign against some species of animals, the zebra, or the pigs, and try and induce all the other animals to drive them away. But if that happened, the result might be that some one species of animals would have a very great deal of power after a time, and it wasn't likely to be the monkeys. The monkeys were speedy and cunning, but they weren't strong, and they couldn't endure great hardships either.

No, Chita decided, the balance of power must not be upset. It wouldn't do to get rid of all of one species. Then he wondered if he could use the people's snobbish instincts. Could he put forward the idea that only the families who had lived in that particular bit

63

of forest for a very long time might remain? A settlement of the oldest and "best" families. But when he examined that notion, it proved to be too complicated. For one thing the bats were certainly among the oldest families in the vicinity but they weren't friendly, they kept themselves to themselves. Then there was the tortoise, his family were long lived, and would perhaps be the oldest of all, but he was a cunning fellow. So were all his relatives. A settlement run by the tortoise clan might be a pretty poor place for everyone else.

Still Chita felt there was something in the idea if only he could work it out. Feeling hungry after so much concentration he went off and found a bunch of bananas for himself, and as he ate he again pondered.

It wouldn't do to get rid of one species, and it wouldn't do to get rid of all but the oldest families. Then what about colour? Suppose all the dark skinned people were made to go, and the light coloured ones remain in control? But that was no use because monkeys were of every shade from white to black. Regretfully Chita abandoned that plan. What else divided people? Ah, he had it at last! Age! The eternal struggle between age and youth. He would start a campaign for the exile of all the old people. He himself was on the sunny side of young manhood, and like most monkeys Chita never gave a thought to the future. The scheme seemed perfect, and the sooner he put it into operation the better.

Finishing the last banana Chita set forth to spread subtle propaganda.

Within a week there was a burning new problem in the bush, and almost only one topic of conversation. The tyranny of age over youth. Youth was not getting a square deal. The old people had done what they liked in the past, but they continued to hold power in the present, and what was the future going to be if things went on like this?

"Look at this question of the best quality food, who gets it?" Chita enquired of a fat young bush pig.

"Well, I don't do so badly," the pig said thoughtfully.

"But you don't do as well as your grandfather," declared Chita.

"How can I?" asked the pig. "After all he's been nosing round here for years longer than I have. He knows all the best places to go."

"Isn't that just what I'm saying," put in Chita eagerly. "If he didn't get hold of the best things first you'd soon find them. It's the advantage of age over youth, that's what it is."

"But," said the pig, and then fell silent. As an argument there was a flaw in it somewhere, but at the same time it was true that if grandfather didn't get there first the young pig would eventually find the place where the best food was to be got. "Maybe you're right," he told Chita.

"Of course I'm right," snapped Chita, and went on to spread his idea elsewhere.

He didn't find it too easy because no one was much interested in ideas anyhow, but with persistence he began to win the day. Naturally nobody was quite satisfied with their lot, and it was satisfactory to pin their troubles on somebody. If the old people could be blamed it didn't seem so depressing as having to blame oneself.

The whole plot was working up nicely by the time Chita encountered the tortoise.

"What I don't understand is how you work out who is old and who isn't," the tortoise commented. "For instance I'm at least twenty times your age, but I'm young as tortoises go. On the other hand the humming bird is only a few months old, but he'll be a grandfather in a year's time."

Chita teetered impatiently.

"I'm talking about the older generation of course, parents, and grandparents. We want to be free of their tyranny."

"You mean you desire to send your own mother into exile?" the tortoise asked.

Chita looked defiant.

"This isn't a personal matter, it's for the good of the community. My mother will have to go with the rest."

"Well, my mother won't," the tortoise said shortly.

"You are shockingly anti-social. I shall report this to my Committee," Chita said angrily.

"Why, have you got a Committee?" the tortoise asked in surprise.

"Naturally, all movements have to have Committees," Chita snapped, and swung off in high dudgeon.

As a matter of fact Chita had no Committee, but he had decided on the spur of the moment that one had to be got together at once.

Getting a Committee together wasn't easy at first. Almost everyone was interested in the promise of getting a lot more food, but no one wanted extra work. But by dark Chita had managed to enrol four members. The young pig, a vulture, a crocodile and a

cobra. Next day he had succeeded in working up their enthusiasm
to a point where they set off to convert their own people to the idea
that everyone who was a parent of an adult should go into exile.

At first the old people and the parents took the thing as a joke,
but by the time another week had passed it was serious. Gradually
all the young people had withdrawn, and formed into hostile
groups who were determined to drive away all parents and older
people. Before the new moon came up the plan had been accom-
plished. Pained and bewildered the oldsters had been driven away,
and the youngsters were left in possession.

Chita had been kept so busy that he had had no time to attend
to details, and he was curious to know how the tortoise had taken
the change, and how he felt about parting from his mother.

"So you are master of your own house at last," Chita commented, when he found the tortoise sitting on the river bank.

"No man is master," the tortoise said slowly.

"How did your mother take the change?" Chita enquired, not
to be deprived of making his point. But the tortoise remained
unmoved.

"We are a philosophical family," he replied with what appeared
to be a shrug of his shoulders under his heavy shell, and he
waddled slowly towards the water.

At first the young people were pleased and excited by the new
situation. They had far more food, more than they could possibly
eat, in fact some of the very young ones became ill, and a few died
as a result of over-eating. This fate overtook the young pig, and
Chita had to find a new member for his Committee. However, it
was easy this time, people were now only too eager to join. Food
was so plentiful that there was very little to do. At first feasts had
been organised, but after a time these palled. Committees were a
new idea, and before long, there were so many Committees that
it was quite bewildering.

The tortoise, sitting peacefully on the river bank as usual one day,
was bowled over by a young crocodile shooting out of the water.

"Where on earth are you going to?" asked the tortoise.

"My Committee meeting," hissed the crocodile.

"What Committee?" asked the tortoise.

"The C.C.C."

"What's that?" enquired the tortoise.

"The Cultural Council of Crocodiles," said the crocodile loftily,
and swished off through the bush with an air of great importance.

"Are you alone?" a quiet voice asked from the roots of a tree. "I'm alone, mother, come out and sit in the sun," replied the tortoise.

The mother of the tortoise came out cautiously, sat on the bank, and sighed.

"Well, well! I never thought I'd see the day when I'd live like a fugitive. You know, son, sometimes I wonder if it wouldn't be best if I went off and joined the other old people."

"Would you prefer it?" asked the tortoise.

"It's hard to say, everything is so strange nowadays, but I feel it might make things easier for you, and after all I'm no use here."

"But you may be," said the tortoise. "Have patience, and stay a bit longer. This silly business can't last. You'll see."

But it did last, and it seemed to last a very long time when one was an old lady forced to live hidden under the roots of a tree. The rainy season had come, and gone, food was plentiful, and life was one long festival for the overfed animals.

"The waste of food is terrible," mourned the old lady, as she chatted with her son. "Whatever will become of them if they don't put by some stores? It's a good thing we don't have droughts here. There hasn't been one since I was a girl. That was a terrible time. I remember we had to eat all sorts of things we had never eaten before, and but for the fact that some very old people had been through droughts before, and knew what strange things were edible we shouldn't have survived. A good many rash people were poisoned, or starved, as it was."

"Get back," whispered her son. "I hear someone coming."

The old lady barely reached the roots of the tree when Chita appeared. He looked round him curiously. Strange tales had been carried to him lately. People reported that the tortoise was surely going out of his mind because he had been overheard talking to himself. At least he must have been talking to himself because when visitors walked in they found the tortoise alone. Chita was not satisfied however. He knew the tortoise was very wise, and cunning, and Chita had never been convinced that the tortoise had really given in to the new regime.

He now assumed an air of surprise.

"Oh, are you alone? I heard voices a moment ago!"

"As you see I am alone," rejoined the tortoise.

"You talk to yourself!" exclaimed Chita.

"I must talk to someone," rejoined the tortoise.

Chita's little red eyes looked suspicious.

"You shouldn't remain alone so much. You should join one of our Committees."

"Why?"

"Well, for one thing people are beginning to talk. You don't mix with any one any more, and it gives a bad impression."

"How is that?" asked the tortoise, drooping his eyelids.

"It looks as if you didn't approve of things as they are now?"

"Would that make any difference?"

"What do you mean?" asked Chita suspiciously.

"Whether I approve or not. Things are going very well. Aren't they?"

"Wonderfully well. That's why we want everyone's support. It would be such a pity if everyone weren't happy and satisfied."

The tortoise closed his eyes as if preparing to doze.

"It would be, wouldn't it," he said lazily.

Flipping his tail with irritation Chita hurried away. At least he pretended to hurry away, but as soon as he got out of sight he slipped back again, and hid behind a tree. He felt sure the tortoise was up to something. But the tortoise was wily, and his mother was no fool. She kept quiet, and the tortoise apparently dozed. After some time he heard very quiet movements. Chita had given up watching and gone home.

The days passed and the animals led a carefree existence. Food was less plentiful than it had been, but the rains were due soon, and nobody worried. All sorts of societies flourished. As well as the Cultured Crocodiles, there were the Philosophical Pigs, who met every Saturday night for a truffle feast, and the Ants' Art Society who were Town Planners, and the crickets who had a Choral Group. There were many others as well, including the Baronial Bipeds Club, organised by Chita himself.

But now a cloud overshadowed the animals' carefree existence, or rather an absence of cloud was the cause for depression, for the rains didn't come, and food became more and more scarce.

"This is the most shocking state of affairs," young Mrs. Zebra complained to Mrs. Doe. "Nothing like it has ever happened in my lifetime. The rains always fell with great regularity."

"None of us remember anything like this," replied Mrs. Doe. "I was telling Mr. Chita that only yesterday. I do wish he'd do something about it, he seems so clever."

"I suggest we appoint a deputation, and go to see him," Mrs. Zebra said, and hurried off to tell all her friends. They all agreed that the deputation was a good idea, and a large crowd got together and went off to Chita's home.

Chita was not there. He had made another of his secret expeditions to spy on the tortoise. He had been doing it for some days. He was almost certain now that the tortoise had someone hidden, and who could that someone be but his mother. Chita was determined to catch the old lady, and make a first class crisis. This would achieve two results, both of them very satisfactory, and secondly a scandal would keep people from thinking so much about the drought.

When Chita crept close to the tortoise's home he was rewarded at last. Heat and thirst had driven old Mrs. Tortoise to the mud of the river bank where she and her son were chatting quietly. Delighted, Chita sped back to his friends, hastily organised them into a band and led them to the river bank. So quietly and cunningly did they move that poor Mrs. Tortoise never sensed their presence until she was surrounded.

"What are you going to do with my mother?" demanded the tortoise, as he glared at the grinning monkeys.

"She is a criminal, and must stand trial. She has broken the law," retorted Chita. Despite all pleas from the tortoise the poor old lady was turned on her back and carried off to be gaoled in Chita's house.

It was not easy to pick a judge and jury from the worried bush folk. They wanted food, not justice. Chita himself acted for the prosecution, and the tortoise undertook to defend his mother.

Chita had been working for days on the case for the prosecution, and the vulture, who was judge, was prepared to agree with everything he said.

"Your Worship," he began. "This old woman has committed the most grievous crime against the State. She has conspired with her son to overthrow the Law. At a great cost to our own feelings we freed ourselves from the shackles imposed on us by the old people in order to win our freedom, to create a community of young people no longer dragged down by the dead weight of the old and useless. You have all seen the wonderful result."

At this a murmur rose in the Court.

"We never had a drought before. How do we know it isn't a punishment for driving away the old people?" someone shouted.

"Silence in the Court," cackled the Judge.

"The voice of superstition," Chita shrilled hastily. "How much worse would be our sufferings during the drought if we had thousands of old people to feed. If we hadn't got rid of them we should have starved by now."

On and on he went until a truly terrifying case had been built up against poor Mrs. Tortoise. At length her son was allowed to speak in her defence, although no one believed his efforts on her behalf could be of any use.

"I don't propose to defend my mother's action in remaining behind. The facts will do that. As far as I know there are only two people who have not suffered great hardship from lack of food in the last week or so. Myself and my mother!"

At this audacious statement a great howl arose.

"Quiet," shouted the tortoise. "The reason we have had food was because my mother knows where to find it. She lived through a drought before, and survived because the old people of that day knew where to look for unknown and strange foods that enabled them to exist until things improved. None of us young people know about these things."

At this his words were drowned. The animals began to break up in wild disorder. "Bring back the old people to save us." "My grandmother would never let me die of hunger." "My mother will be able to help us." "My father was a clever man, he'll know about this." "My grandfather was the oldest person in the bush, he'll know where to find food."

So they all clamoured, and began to run wildly in the direction they had despatched the old people months before. No one was left but the vulture and Chita, and no one was prepared to listen to them any more. "Court adjourned," croaked the vulture weakly, and flapped his way across the tree tops. There was always a chance that someone might have been trampled to death in the rush to find the old people.

The tortoise and his mother made their way home, and sat quietly on the river bank. They enjoyed a very peaceful time for several days because it took the others a long time to find their exiled relatives, and even when they did find them there was a good deal of explaining to do. Most of the old people forgave their children, however, and came back, and helped them to find food until the rains came. Chita's mother, and all his ancient relatives, and there were many of them, were the exceptions. Monkeys are rather bad tempered, vindictive people, and have long memories. That is why, to this very day such awful quarrels go on among the monkey folk.

THE SNAKE IN THE FOREST

In almost every village in West Africa there is a story about some animal, reptile, or bird, which has been living in the neighbourhood for a very long time, such as a crocodile, a tortoise, or a snake, as these creatures live to a very old age.

This is a story about a snake who had lived for such a long time that no one could remember when he first appeared. Because he was old, and cunning, and very large, all sorts of tales grew up around him, and many people were very frightened of him. It seems, however, that many of these stories were much exaggerated, for there is no real proof that he ever did anyone any great harm. In fact he often did a good turn, as you will hear from the story of Yere and the snake.

Yere was a pretty girl, and everyone said she would certainly make a very successful marriage, and right enough when the time came she married Sako, who was a strong and handsome young man, and a fine worker, and there seemed to be every hope that the marriage would be most blissful.

This alas was not to be. Before a year had passed a new girl named Tinou came to live in the village with her aunt. Tinou was an extraordinarily beautiful girl, she was also sly and lazy. She had resolved to make a good marriage, but it seemed to her that the most attractive man in the village was already married, because Sako was the one man she wanted. Now it is the custom in some parts of Africa for a man to have several wives if he can afford to keep them, so Tinou resolved to try and induce Sako to make her his second wife.

So every day the wicked Tinou made some opportunity to talk to Sako, and gradually they became more and more friendly, until after some months had passed, Sako decided he would marry

71

Tinou. This upset Yere terribly but it was not until the marriage had taken place that she realised what a very bad thing it was. Once Tinou was married she used all her cunning to make Yere miserable, because she wanted to get rid of her.

Sako had no idea of the truth of matters because he was very busy, and he was quite bemused by Tinou, and thought Yere was making things worse than need be. Gradually Tinou poisoned his mind until poor Yere found that her position was worse than that of a slave. So she stayed at home, and moped, and wept, while Tinou went with Sako to feasts and dances. All the good things went to Tinou and not to Yere. Good food, fine clothes, jewellery, and everything else that was to be got.

So Yere became almost an outcast, and spent much of her time wandering in the forest, weeping. One day she was particularly unhappy because there was to be a great feast, and she had no new clothes. She decided she would stay away rather than appear in her old ones, while Tinou openly triumphed over her.

So she ran away to hide her grief in the lonely forest. She was sitting sobbing on a tree trunk when she heard a voice.

"What are you crying for?" the voice asked, in the low harsh tones of a very old man.

Yere looked round but could see nobody. Then near her feet she saw a large snake, watching her with strange beady eyes that looked as if they knew everything.

Between her sobs Yere told the snake about the cruel way Tinou and Sako treated her. "Now," she ended, "all the neighbours know about it, and I am not going to the feast in my old clothes to be shamed before everyone."

"Can't you get any new clothes?" enquired the snake.

"No, Tinou takes everything, and pretends that I am sulking and don't want to have new clothes."

"Why don't you explain to your husband?" asked the snake.

"Because I have some pride. I've tried to explain, but it's no use. He just thinks I'm jealous."

"I suppose you are too," said the snake.

"Of course I am. Who wouldn't be, but if he would treat me more fairly I'd put up with it. It's the Law that a man can have two wives, but it's not the Law that one should be made a Queen and the other a slave."

The snake shook himself impatiently, and the sound was like dry leaves blowing along the ground.

"You people can be very silly and cruel," he told Yere. "These things don't happen between snakes."

"I suppose not, but what can I do? I'm not a snake."

"All the worse for you!"

The snake became thoughtful.

"What do you want to do? Go to the party in a fine dress and make Tinou sick with envy, and try and make your husband like you again?"

Yere nodded. "That's what I want to do, but I haven't got a dress, so I can't."

"You come along with me," the snake said in such a firm voice that Yere could do nothing but follow him as he slid away through the grass. After they had gone a short distance the snake suddenly began to disappear; first his head, then his body, and then the tip of his tail vanished. Yere gazed helplessly after him. Why had she been so silly as to believe a snake, everyone knew they weren't to be trusted. Tears rolled down her cheeks once more.

"Come, come," she heard the dry voice say. "Don't stand there crying. Stoop down and wriggle in."

Yere then saw that a small bush had been bent by the passing of a heavy body. She found that behind the bush there was a hole between some rocks. The hole was just large enough for her to wriggle through. Down, down she went, into the dark, and once more she wondered if she had been tricked. Then quite suddenly, it was light again, and she was in a large cave, lit from a gap in the rocks high above.

Yere gazed around in amazement. The walls of the cave seemed to be hung with gleaming cloth all the colours of the rainbow. Yere looked at these bright, beautiful strips, and gaped.

"Pretty good, aren't they?" chuckled the snake. "Those are *my* old clothes, but they are a lot better than yours, aren't they?"

"They are beautiful!" Yere gasped. "Much more beautiful than any clothes I've seen before."

"Of course they are. Now take your choice. Pick out one to wear at the feast."

"You mean you're going to give me one?"

The snake shook his head.

"That might cause trouble in the end. I'll lend you one."

"Oh, thank you, thank you!" Yere sobbed.

"You'll thank me best by drying your tears, looking pretty and cheerful again so that you can do my clothes credit and have a good time at the feast. Now, which one will you choose?"

Yere walked round fingering the beautiful skins, and finally chose one that seemed to hold all the colours of the setting sun.

"This one, please," Yere said humbly. "When shall I bring it back?"

"Bring it back at sunset in three days' time, and if it's in good order you may have the loan of it again some time, or of any of the others."

Yere felt overcome with gratitude.

"Oh, thank you, thank you. You are very good to me."

"I don't like people crying round my forest disturbing my afternoon nap. It's uncomfortable. If you think wearing my old skin is likely to make things better, then I can have my nap in peace."

"Oh, I'm sure it will," Yere asssured him. "And I'll take great care of your skin."

The snake puffed himself a little.

"You'd better. If you don't I shall be very, very cross. I've never lent anything to anyone before."

Yere slipped away and walked through the forest as if on air. Help had certainly come from an unexpected quarter, and she pinned all her hopes on the idea that if only her husband could see her as he used to do, looking beautiful, and carefree, he would cease to neglect her.

Yet she felt that in taking the snake skin she was taking a risk also. Ever since she was a little girl she had heard about the ancient, mysterious snake, who was so powerful. Suppose some accident befell the dress, what then? She was perfectly well aware that if Tinou knew about the skin she would destroy it if she got the chance.

Yere stopped when she reached the edge of the village. It was deserted; the people had not yet come back from their farms. Yere slipped quickly to her hut, hid the snakeskin, and then set about preparing supper. She could hide the skin but she could not hide the light in her eyes, and Tinou looked at her curiously as she went about her tasks.

"Where did you spend the afternoon?" asked Tinou, wondering what had happened to make Yere cheerful. "Oh, I just went for a walk in the forest," Yere replied. "You spend a lot of time in the forest," Tinou remarked. "Perhaps you have friends there?"

"Perhaps I have," Yere answered airily. She felt quite safe because no one ever went to the remote corner where the snake lived; everyone was too much afraid of him.

Still Tinou was not satisfied. She could scarcely eat her supper for wondering what it was that had caused Yere to change from someone utterly crushed to a cheerful girl again. "Anyhow she won't dare to come to the feast in her old rags, and even if she does Sako won't notice her. Maybe I can manage to do something to provoke her, and then Sako will send her back to her own people in disgrace. Then I'll be his first, and only wife," thought Tinou.

Sako had come in late to supper, and he was too hurried to notice any change in Yere, even if he had had eyes for her, which he had not. By this time he had come to believe that Tinou's criticisms of Yere were true, that she was jealous and ill-humoured, and that perhaps he had made a mistake in marrying her in the first place.

After supper Yere went quietly to her hut, and sat there waiting for the others to go to the feast. Soon she heard them pass.

"Where is Yere? Isn't she coming?" she heard Sako ask Tinou.

"She said she didn't want to come. She was quite disagreeable about it," lied Tinou. "It's better for her to remain at home as she's so disagreeable."

"Perhaps I'd better go in and speak to her," Sako suggested.

"Why should you bother," Tinou asked swiftly. "Let us forget about her, and be happy. You know she only makes you miserable," and she seized his hand, and dragged him along the path.

Tears started to Yere's eyes, but she fought them back. Then she bathed, and dressed her hair, put on what ornaments Tinou had left her, and lastly draped herself in the snakeskin. Then she set off for the feast.

By this time the feast was at its height, and Tinou felt very satisfied with herself. She was the most beautiful woman there. All the other women envied her, and no one spoke of Yere. Sako also seemed to have completely forgotten his first wife. "Yere might just as well not exist," Tinou told herself triumphantly.

Suddenly there was silence, and Tinou looked round to see what had happened. A woman was standing in the firelight. A woman who made everyone stare and gasp because she was so beautiful. She was dressed in clothes such as no one had ever seen before. Her dress seemed to reflect all the colours of the firelight, almost as if she were covered in jewels.

"Why it's Yere," Tinou whispered in amazement. Sako was so surprised that he rose to his feet and went towards her, which made Tinou furious. Then the others began to crowd round Yere also, telling her how beautiful she was, and how pleased they were to see her looking well once more.

Sako led her to the fire, and everyone made much of her. After this had gone on for some time Tinou became furious. She rushed at Yere and shouted, "Where did you get the dress? Did you steal it, or did you steal something from my husband to obtain it? It is disgraceful that the wife of a farmer should wear such clothes."

"I came by the dress honestly," Yere said quietly. "Sako's goods have not paid for it."

"I don't believe you," screamed Tinou. "Sako, send her home. She is lying."

At this the people began to murmur because they had known Yere all their lives, and they did not believe that she would do anything dishonourable. Besides one did not make scenes at a feast.

"We have no wish that Yere should go," said an old woman. "If you cannot keep your temper, Tinou, it would be better for you to go."

"Very well," flared Tinou. "Come, Sako!"

But Sako was displeased by her bad manners.

"I will come in good time. I think it best that you go now," he told her and walked away. Tinou could do nothing but go home by herself. When she had gone Sako walked back and sat by Yere. He found her very beautiful, and very pleasant company, and he began to realise that he had misjudged her, and that he had allowed Tinou to influence him overmuch. He did not know it, but for the first time since he had seen Tinou, he was free from her spell. In halting tones he tried to tell Yere how sorry he was for the way he had treated her. The neighbours also felt that they had neglected Yere lately so everyone tried to make amends, and the feast went on merrily. Everyone ate, drank, danced, and enjoyed themselves thoroughly.

At the end Sako walked home with Yere, and promised her that she would always be treated as chief wife in future, and that if Tinou did not treat her with respect he would send Tinou home to her family. In short Yere's plan to regain her place in Sako's affections seemed to have completely succeeded. Because she was kind and gentle Yere told Sako she was sure that the second wife had not really meant to be unkind, and that they must all try and live happily together.

This wish, however, was unshared by Tinou. She had arrived home in such a rage that she had torn up everything in the hut that she could tear, and smashed all the cooking pots. Then she lay raging and biting her nails. For a time she hoped Sako would follow her, but when she heard him walk home with Yere her fury knew no bounds, and she resolved to have revenge on Yere whatever happened.

She got up quietly, and listened to Sako talking to Yere.

"Perhaps I had better tell you where got this beautiful dress," Yere was saying, and then she told Sako the whole story of the snake. When Tinou heard this she knew she had just the chance she wanted.

The powerful snake was famous. Everyone feared and respected him. Lots of people even left offerings for him in the forest. Tinou had never done this because she was too greedy, and also too cowardly to go near his lair. This was not really surprising because many a man who had tried to penetrate into the lair, and steal the cast off skins had been killed. Tinou felt certain that if only she could destroy the skin Yere would be killed also.

So she waited until Yere was asleep, and then crept into the hut. She took a chopper and the snakeskin, and went a little way into the bush. Here she chopped the skin to pieces. It then occurred to her that if Yere was too terrified to take back the pieces to the snake he might take revenge on the whole village, and she did not want to be there when he came. So she packed all her possessions. When Sako waked she was all ready to leave.

"I am going away on a visit to my Uncle," she told him. "I am very much hurt and offended at what ocurred last night, and I prefer to go away for a time."

She fully expected Sako to try and dissuade her, but he was only too pleased with this temporary solution of the trouble between his two wives, and much to Tinou's annoyance he said a visit to her Uncle seemed a very good idea. Tinou was in no way pleased at this, but there was nothing she could do but go, so off she went.

Yere rose full of hope and happiness, and set about preparing food for her husband. When she had tidied the hut she went to look at the snakeskin, and then she discovered it had gone. In dismay she rushed outside, and there lying on the ground were the fragments of the skin. Yere cried out, and sank to her knees. Hearing her cry Sako came to see what was the matter.

"Oh look," cried Yere. "The snake's beautiful skin. He trusted me with it, and now look what has befallen. Tinou found it and has chopped it into pieces. Oh, I should have taken better care of it. The snake will never forgive me."

Hearing the commotion the villagers came out, and Sako and Yere told them the whole story of the snakeskin.

"You must not take it back, Yere. The snake might kill you."

"Oh, but I must," said Yere. "Don't you see he trusted me."

"If she doesn't take it back he will come and look for her," said an old man.

"She could hide," suggested Sako.

"If she does that he might wreck the whole village," the old man told them.

"Then I shall take it," said Sako.

Yere cried out against this.

"It is only fair that he should," said the old man. "After all none of these things would have happened if he had not taken a second wife."

"Let Tinou take it back then," someone else shouted. "She was the one who destroyed it. She was the one who caused all the trouble. Where is she?"

"She has gone," said Sako. "Gone on a visit to her Uncle."

"The traitoress. She guessed that the snake might take revenge on us all."

While they were talking Yere gathered the snakeskin up in her arms, and turned towards the forest.

"Stop," cried Sako. "You must not go."

"I must go," said Yere. "I know Tinou was to blame, but I know that you, Sako, are partly to blame, but I feel I am most of all to blame. I should not have borrowed the skin in the first place. If the snake kills me it cannot be helped."

"But I can't let you go," protested her husband.

"You must let me go," said Yere.

"No, I am coming also," said Sako.

"We cannot let our friends go alone," cried the old man. "Let us all go."

So they all formed themselves into a very sad procession and set off through the forest. When they came to the cleft in the rocks Yere firmly refused to allow them to come any further.

"You made me very happy," she told them. "And so have you Sako. But this is my business, and I have to go through with it myself. Whatever happens I am not unhappy because I know I have your love and confidence."

With that she slipped into the crack between the rocks, and disappeared. Sako and the villagers fell on their faces and wept.

Through the dark tunnel went Yere, and then into the light.

"May I come in?" she called out.

"Why, of course," replied the snake in surprise. He regarded Yere curiously while stammering and sobbing she told him what had happened, and showed him the tattered skin.

"I don't suppose you will believe me," she ended. "I suppose you think I was careless, and left the skin where Tinou could get at it easily, but I didn't. Now do what you will. Kill me if you like, but don't hurt Sako or my people."

The snake had been puffing himself larger and larger while Yere spoke, and his eyes gleamed red with rage. Now he stopped still, as if carved in stone. Yere thought him the most terrifying thing she had ever seen. She hid her eyes, and gave herself up for lost. Her heart beat so loudly that she could scarcely hear the snake when he began to speak.

"I believe you," he told her. "I believe you because very little goes on that I don't know about. Tinou was vengeful, and greedy. You know she never once left me an offering. I shall see that she pays for it all now."

"You aren't going to kill her?" Yere gasped.

"Not if she stays where she is now—she won't like that. But if she ever attempts to come back to these parts again I shall certainly kill her!"

"And what about me? I am quite willing to accept all the blame," said Yere. "But please spare my husband and my people."

"What do you think I am?" asked the snake. "A human being? Why should I be so stupid as to want to punish your husband and your neighbours?"

"Oh, thank you," said Yere. "Thank you. Do with me what you will."

"I am getting old and lazy," replied the snake. "I think I should like some more offerings, more often. I charge you to see that I get them."

"You mean you are going to let me go?" exclaimed Yere.

"Yes, you aren't to blame for the loss of my skin—and it was only my second best skin anyhow," the snake added slyly.

Yere jumped joyfully to her feet.

"Oh, you're wonderful. I'm so happy. I'm the happiest person in the world, and I owe everything to you!"

The snake glowed pink with embarrassment, right from his jaws to the tip of his tail. Yere stared at him in amazement.

"That's right," he said gruffly. "It's been a pleasure. If you want the loan of another dress sometime, just let me know. Only don't overdo it."

With a last cry of thanks Yere turned towards the tunnel, ran through it as fast as she could, and came out to find Sako and the people with their faces on the ground, crying.

She laughed and cried all at once, and told them what had happened. They showered thanks on the snake, and set off back to the village greatly rejoicing.

As their voices died away the snake curled up comfortably. The blush faded out of his jaws, and out of his body, and the last gleam of it flickered away in his tail. He was all green and gold once more. He felt very content. As he dozed off to sleep he reminded himself that next time he saw Yere he must remind her that all snakes were not like him. It didn't do to get *too* friendly with snakes.

THE GREEDY MONKEY

LIFE IN THE jungle is never easy. Animals and birds have to keep very busy in order to feed themselves and their families. Usually they find enough food, but sometimes, owing to drought or floods, no one has enough to eat.

Once there was a particularly severe drought, and the jungle folk suffered severe hardships. They roved for miles to find sufficient to keep them alive. One of the most persistent food hunters was a monkey. She was very fond of food herself, and also prided herself on being a very good housewife, and mother. Her name was Mala. Mala had a baby of whom she was very proud. It had a beautiful shiny coat and Mala believed this was because she always managed to include palm nuts in the baby's diet. Mala was very clever about finding these nuts, and she set off early every morning, leaving her husband at home to mind the baby.

One day, after travelling for miles, Mala had almost given up in despair, when she at last came across a palm with a few nuts on it. In her eagerness to gather them as quickly as possible, she dropped one. Being such a careful housewife, she hated to think the nut might be wasted, and slid down the tree so quickly, that she reached the ground at the same time as the falling nut. To her disgust the nut rolled into a hole. Determined not to lose the nut Mala scrambled in after it. Ahead of her she could hear the nut rolling down further and further. Undaunted she followed. Still the nut went on, and Mala realised that this was no ordinary hole she had found, but a long tunnel leading down into the depths of the earth.

Some people might have become nervous, and turned back, but not Mala the monkey. When there was a possibility of food Mala was not to be put off by darkness, or even danger. So on and on she went, and then suddenly the tunnel came to an end.

Beyond the tunnel Mala saw a clearing with beautiful green grass, trees full of fruit, and flowers, and beyond a lovely river sparkling in the sunlight. Some of the trees and fruits Mala had seen before, but many others were quite unfamiliar. In the clearing many animals, looking very well fed, were gambolling cheerily. All this was so unexpected, and so unlike the world Mala had left up above that she paused in sheer amazement.

The pause lost her the nut she had been following for it rolled out of the hole on to the ground, and a small monkey playing by himself, picked it up, and proceeded to eat it.

With a screech of dismay Mala leapt out of the hole, and began to chatter angrily. Startled by her sudden appearance and the noise she was making, the baby monkey dropped the nut. But he had already taken a big bite out of it. Mala began to weep.

As she wept the animals began to gather round and asked anxiously what ailed her. Tearfully Mala told the story of the famine in the world above, how she had been hunting for a nut for her baby, and how the nut had rolled down the hole. How she had bravely followed, and the nut had been spoiled by the baby monkey.

On hearing this the animals became very sympathetic, invited Mala in, offered her a meal, and asked for further information about the world above. Mala told them all she knew, and asked if the drought had not affected them. They said it had not, and then Mala gradually learned that they never had droughts or floods in this wonderful country, never anything but sunshine or gentle rain, and food was always plentiful.

Mala sat back in amazement and envy. No one liked good food better than she did, and a country where food was never scarce seemed like Paradise. She could think of no more glorious prospect than living in a place where she could eat as much as she wanted at any hour of the day or night. She was astounded that her hosts seemed to take their blessings casually, but wishing to appear just as casual as they were she chatted about the beauties of the scenery instead of dwelling on the subject of food. She was quite sure that she had told her hosts quite sufficient about that, to ensure that they wouldn't allow her to go away empty-handed.

She was therefore greatly chagrined when the time came to leave that the subject of food was not mentioned. The only present she received was a very large and handsome drum. Mala did her best to seem tremendously grateful for this fine but useless gift and started off home feeling very dispirited.

When she arrived home her husband and baby were waiting very anxiously. They were much disappointed when they found she had no food, and far too hungry to take much interest in the tale of her strange adventure in the wonderful world under the ground.

"Are you sure you didn't fall asleep and dream it all?" her husband asked.

"I did not," Mala said indignantly. "Here is proof; look at this splendid drum they gave me!"

"I wish they had given you a few nuts instead," her husband complained, and gave the drum a kick. Immediately there was a strange rattle inside the drum.

"Why there is something in it," Mala exclaimed, and rushing to the drum she struck it as hard as she could. As she did so food of all kinds began to fall from the inside of the drum.

Chattering with joy and excitement the three of them leapt on the food, and began to consume it as fast as they could.

The noise of the drum had attracted all the animals in the vicinity, and they peered curiously through the trees, and then hurried forward when they saw all the food.

"Has it fallen from the skies?" asked a wise old tortoise.

"Some friends gave it to me," Mala explained. All the animals gazed at her in awe, and Mala suddenly realised that she had become a person of great importance. Greedy as she was for food, Mala was greedy for popularity also.

"There is plenty for everyone," she told them. "Get ready for a feast!"

Immediately the animals broke into a great hubbub, and hurried around making preparations.

"Do you think it wise to let everyone eat as much as they like?" the tortoise asked Mala. "Wouldn't it be better to give everyone a little at a time? The food would then last much longer."

But Mala only looked at him scornfully. Never before had she been in a position to shine socially, and she felt far too exalted to listen to reason.

"There is plenty more where that came from," she said loftily. The tortoise shook his head doubtfully, and retired under his shell.

For the next two days Mala was the most popular person in the jungle. Everyone made merry, everyone was very grateful to Mala, and very flattering. But after that food began to run short, and finally it was all gone. Mala found she was no longer an important person, worse still she and her family were hungry once more. The same miserable routine of hunting round for food went on, and the drought showed no sign of ending.

"Why don't you go back to your powerful friends for more food?" asked Mala's husband.

"I will very soon," Mala snapped, and pretended to be very busy about her toilet. Although she would never have admitted it, Mala actually felt a little nervous about going back to the underworld again. The people there had seemed so wise and sensible. No one had boasted as Mala and her friends did, no one had chattered unnecessarily, no one had quarrelled. No one had shown the least desire to create any false impression. The way in which they had bestowed the food on her showed the delicacy of their feelings. Still perhaps it was easy to show all these good qualities when you lived in a world where there was no hunger. "But," came the uneasy thought, "why didn't you act as the tortoise suggested? Why did you squander the food? If the people in the underworld knew about that would they be so generous another time?" Mala lacked the courage to find out.

As the days passed Mala thought hard and finally hit upon a plan. She decided to go back to the underworld again, but to make her visit appear accidental. So early one morning she set off. When she arrived at the palm tree over the entrance to the tunnel, she searched anxiously for a palm nut, and eventually found one. Carrying it very carefully to the ground she deliberately rolled it down the hole, and then went after it. Down, down through the long dark tunnel went Mala, and the nut went rolling along before her. At last she saw light ahead.

To her relief the wonderful world under the ground looked just the same. The sun shone, the trees, and flowers glittered, and there were nuts and fruit in abundance. The same little monkey was playing around the opening of the tunnel, and to Mala's joy, when the nut rolled out he pounced on it once more, and began to eat. As soon as she saw this Mala, uttering a loud cry ran out. Immediately a crowd gathered round.

"Woe, woe," cried Mala. "Once again the nut I had for my child has been taken from me?"

"How did it get here?" cried someone in the crowd.

"Just as it did before," wailed Mala. "There is still famine above the ground. I hunted and hunted for nuts. I found none until I reached the tree above the tunnel. Then I saw one, and in my eagerness I dropped it, and it rolled down here."

"Have you really had nothing to eat lately?" asked a wise old owl. "Nothing. For myself I do not mind, it is my poor baby I worry about," said Mala.

For a while there was silence and everyone stared at Mala. She felt that they were reading her mind, and wondered if they guessed how she had squandered the food they gave her.

"I must thank you for your gift last time I was here," she said hastily. "It was wonderful, but of course I had to share it with everyone, and it is long since gone!"

They listened to her without comment, and the owl invited her to sit down, and food was brought to her. Mala felt that all was well, and she had no more to fear. She felt sure that they would not let her go away empty-handed, and she began to wonder if she could not even do better still. Why should she and her family continue to starve in the world above, while down here everyone lived in luxury.

"Never in my life have I seen any place so beautiful as this," Mala remarked to the owl. "Your trees and flowers are so fine. I am so sensitive to beauty, far more so than my friends up above. My tastes are really refined, and so are my husband's, and our baby is a sensitive and clever little fellow. We would willingly leave the world above, if you could spare us a corner down here. We should be so happy in these beautiful surroundings, and among such charming people."

"The owl looked at her solemnly and shook his head. "That is impossible. No one may come to live here unless they have been selected."

Piqued, but trying to be beautifully polite, Mala looked sad. "Then couldn't we be selected? How is it done? Is it like a Club? Do we have to be elected?"

"Yes, in a way," replied the owl.

"Oh, I do wish you would tell me how to set about it?" Mala exclaimed.

"No, that is forbidden. I am sorry, I must leave you now, I have things to do," the owl said rather shortly, and flapped quietly away.

Very upset at this Mala turned her attention to other people, and from each of them she tried tactfully to extract the information as to how she and her family could gain permission to live in this lovely underworld. In each case she failed. The secret was evidently closely guarded. Not even the most heart-rending references to the distress in the world above, and the distress of her family in particular, could gain Mala a clue.

"The drought must soon be over, and you will all have food again," they told her. Disgruntled Mala decided to return home. At least they would have to give her a parting gift.

So Mala made her farewells, and once more as she prepared to leave, a large drum was brought in, the owl flapping around it. Mala gave most effusive thanks, shouldered the drum, and set off up the tunnel.

No longer admiring, but jealous and resentful, Mala made her way home. She decided that these people must be snobs, and after all she and her family were just as good any day. Well, never mind, at least she had secured another load of food. Her trick had worked.

When she arrived home Mala found a large crowd waiting for her. They had guessed that she must be visiting her mysterious and powerful friends, and were in a state of great excitement anticipating another feast.

When they saw Mala they surged round her, cheering, and clapping her on the back. At first Mala was in no way pleased. She would have preferred to hoard all the food for herself and her family this time. It would be very unwise to feast recklessly again. But seeing the expectant eyes around her, listening to their compliments, Mala was unable to resist another opportunity to be a person of great importance if only for a few days.

"Here is plenty of food for everyone!" she cried dumping the drum on the ground.

"Surely you aren't going to have another feast?" hissed the tortoise.

"Why not," cried Mala recklessly. "The drought will soon be over anyhow!"

The crowd cheered loudly and pressed around the drum.

"Let me beat it!" cried Mala's husband, and began forthwith to belabour the drum.

But no rattle of fruit and nuts rewarded his efforts. Instead came a strange rustling sound, and from inside the drum swarmed legions of tiny, strange creatures such as no one had ever seen before. They hovered over the crowd which immediately began to vanish in all directions until no one was left in the clearing but Mala and her family.

Calling for revenge on the people of the underworld Mala sat down and wept. She was hungry and disappointed, and worse still humiliated because the people of the underworld had evidently seen through her trick, and tried to teach her a lesson.

As Mala and her family wept rain began to mingle with their tears. The drought had ended.

"Rain, rain," cried Mala. "Now we need fear no longer, in a little while there will be plenty of food!"

True there was soon food, but there were other things too. Everyone began to fall ill, and with illnesses such as had never been known before. Disease had been let loose from the drum, and spread all over the earth, and since then all the people and animals in the world have been subject to ills of all kinds such as had never been known until the monkey brought them from the underworld.

THE LEOPARD HAS NO FRIENDS

THE TORTOISE IS a clever and cunning fellow, and one particular tortoise named Basso who lived near the banks of the Benue river, was very clever indeed. During the season when fish were plentiful, he went fishing every day, and returned with a heavy load. He was determined not to share any of his catch with the neighbours, and in particular he was determined that the leopard, who had a very large appetite, should have none. So after he caught his fish, he hid his rod, and took the fish home on his back in a large, covered basket nearly as big as himself.

On his way home he often saw the leopard in the distance. For some days the leopard looked curiously at the basket, but didn't come near, and the tortoise pretended not to see him. At last, however, the leopard became very curious, and stopped the tortoise.

"Can I help you with your load?" he asked politely, his magnificent whiskers twitching with eagerness.

The tortoise shook his head. "No, thank you, I can manage."

"But really I should like to help. I see you carrying these heavy loads so often, and I feel someone should lend aid. Let me carry it a little way."

"No, I really couldn't think of it," the tortoise protested.

"But I insist. We must be good neighbours," the leopard said firmly.

The tortoise looked very sad, and two large tears rolled out of his eyes as he shook his head again.

"I really can't allow you to do that. You see I have a relative here. A dead relative. I am about to bury him!"

The leopard looked shocked.

"My dear fellow, I'm so sorry. How very painful for you. Not a close relative I hope?"

"A cousin," the tortoise said with a catch in his voice.

"Was it sudden?" the leopard enquired.

"Yes, quite sudden."

The leopard looked sympathetic, and then horrified.

"I say, you don't mean to tell me that every time I've seen you with this great basket you are burying a relative?"

The tortoise gave a well-timed sob and nodded.

"I'm afraid so. My poor family seem to be unlucky."

"But I saw you yesterday, and on last Thursday, and twice the week before that," exclaimed the leopard.

The tortoise looked stricken, as indeed he was when he realised how closely the leopard had been watching him.

"That is true. My parents, my uncle, my aunt, and now my poor cousin. All gone."

The leopard backed away a little.

"I say it's nothing catching, is it? I mean, if it is, you yourself—that is any one of us, might catch it."

The tortoise felt alarmed. It would never do if he were forced to leave a neighbourhood where the fishing was so good.

"No, it's nothing infectious," he said hastily. "It's something in the family. We just die off like leaves in the dry season—simply like leaves. Ah, well, I mustn't burden you with my troubles, so I'll be getting along."

But the leopard blocked his path.

"No, my dear fellow. No! You have had all this grief, and none of us have helped. Now that I know about it I insist on helping. Here, give me the basket, and I'll carry it a little way."

Before the tortoise could prevent it the leopard shouldered the basket.

"Which way?" he enquired.

Fuming, the tortoise led the way. He brought up every argument he could think of to induce the leopard to abandon the basket, but the more he protested the more obstinate the leopard became. The tortoise was so perturbed that without noticing he led the leopard round in a circle, and they came back to the spot where they met.

Then the leopard became suspicious.

"Surely this is very strange. Do you mean to bury your cousin here?"

"Yes!" the tortoise said in despair, brokenhearted at the idea of his beautiful fish going under the grimy earth.

"All right," said the leopard, putting down the basket, and proceeding to dig a grave with his great claws. Then he dragged the basket towards the hole. This was too much for the greedy tortoise.

"Stop!" he wailed. "Stop!"

"What is it now?" asked the leopard.

The tortoise looked miserable.

"I'll tell you the truth. That isn't my cousin in the basket."

"Then your cousin isn't dead?"

"I don't know. I haven't seen him for the past twenty years."

"Or your uncle, or your aunt?"

"No, they've gone down the Niger for a change of air."

"And your parents?"

"They celebrated their diamond wedding last week."

"Then what's in the basket?"

"Fish. Very special fish. You see, I'm on a fish diet."

"You mean you put yourself on a fish diet," the leopard retorted grimly.

"Well, why not? It's good for the brain, and it's not easy work catching fish, it needs patience and perseverance."

"And you decided not to share any fish with your neighbours?"

The tortoise looked righteous.

"Why should I? Most of them are lazy fellows. I didn't see why I should feed them. In your case it's different of course. It was most kind of you to offer to help me as you did, and I shall be very pleased to share my fish with you."

"That's very generous of you," the leopard said dryly.

"Not at all. I'm only too delighted. Wait till you taste my special fish stew."

"What's so special about it?" the leopard asked.

"The spices and herbs, my dear fellow. Now look here, I'll take the fish home and get it ready and you go and fetch me some herbs for flavouring—the best ones are in that sunny patch behind the village, and then we'll have a fine feed."

The leopard looked suspicious, but he went, for he knew where to find the tortoise if the fellow tried to cheat him, and he could crush him like a fly. He congratulated himself on his own cleverness. He had suspected that the tortoise was up to something all along, and now he had the tortoise in his power.

The tortoise heaved a sigh of relief as he saw the leopard lope off. It was all nonsense about the special herbs, of course, but herbs wouldn't do any harm, and they did grow where he had told the leopard to go. While the leopard was away he'd have time to think out some new scheme to prevent the leopard sharing the fish.

When the leopard came back with the herbs, the tortoise had a big pot smoking over the fire, and from it came a delicious odour of fish.

"Ah, the herbs," the tortoise gushed. "And what splendid ones. What a banquet we shall have!" Lovingly he dropped in little bits of herbs, and sniffed the steam as if it were perfume.

The leopard stretched himself out and purred with content-ment. This fish diet idea was a good one. In future the tortoise could go fishing every day, but not for himself. "*I'll* have a special fish diet, and the tortoise can have the left-overs," the leopard assured himself.

But the tortoise was thinking furiously, until at last a plan came to him.

"Look here," he suggested. "Why not come for a walk before dinner? It will give us an appetite."

"Why not?" the leopard replied agreeably, and away they strolled into the forest.

"Have you ever played 'Black is White?'" the tortoise asked after a while.

The leopard looked curious.

"Why no, I've never heard of it."

"Well the rules are simple. The thing to remember is that what-ever you *say*, you really *do* the opposite. Suppose you tie me to a tree. I cry out, 'Tie me tighter, tighter!' and you say, 'Tighter, tighter,' but you really make the ropes looser. If I cry 'Looser, looser' you shout 'Looser,' but you tie me tighter."

"It sounds silly," said the leopard. "It's too simple."

"It only sounds simple," the tortoise assured him. "It's really a very clever game, because it's surprising what you do when you get excited."

"Nonsense," said the leopard. "I'm sure I could play that game for hours and hours without ever making a mistake."

"All right," said the tortoise. "Let's try. Here is a tree. There is a liana. Now you pull it down, and I'll let you tie me up."

"Idiotic," grunted the leopard, but proceeded to pull down the rope-like liana, and tied the tortoise to a tree.

"Looser, looser," cried the tortoise. The leopard smirked, and tied the ropes tighter. "Tighter, tighter," squeaked the tortoise, and the leopard growled, "Tighter, tighter," but loosed the ropes.

"Pretty good," commented the tortoise after the game had gone on for ten minutes without the leopard making a single mistake, although he had got a bit breathless.

"It's child play," sniffed the leopard.

"Now let's see if I'm as good as you," the tortoise suggested.

"If you must," said the leopard impatiently, and leaned against a large tree, to which the tortoise proceeded to rope him in no uncertain fashion, until the leopard panted for breath.

"Looser, looser," he gasped, completely forgetting the rules of the game. The tortoise cried "Looser, looser," but pulled the ropes more tightly until the leopard couldn't move an inch. Then he went up to the helpless leopard and smirked.

"You've lost the game. You've lost the dinner."

"Oh, bother the dinner," the leopard snorted. "Let me out of here."

"I think you're better where you are. Good-bye," said the tortoise.

"Come back, come back, enough of this nonsense. You can't leave me here."

"Oh, can't I," carolled the tortoise.

"I'll die of hunger and thirst," shrieked the leopard.

"Probably," said the tortoise, and turned and walked away back to his dinner. The biggest and best dinner he had ever eaten, in his long life. "Brains before brawn," he said derisively, as he thought of the leopard tied to the tree.

Back in the forest the leopard first growled ferociously, and struggled madly. When that proved hopeless he whined pitifully. All the animals in the forest came fearfully and peeped cautiously to see what all the noise was about.

"Free, free me," cried the leopard to a little antelope. But the antelope kicked up its heels and ran, nothing would induce it to go near the leopard, its age-old enemy. "Chew off the ropes, I'll die of thirst," the leopard implored the zebra. But the zebra shook its head and trotted off. It knew the leopard of old. It was the same with the bush pigs who ran away squeaking, and the bush cow, a ferocious beast who had fought with the leopard before now, or even the giant bats. The leopard had no friends.

It was almost dark when the leopard heard a small squeaky voice at his feet. It was a kinkajou, a small animal that comes out at night.

"What's the matter?" squeaked the kinkajou.

"Can't you see I'm tied here, dying of hunger, and thirst. Untie me!" commanded the leopard.

"If I do you'll kill me," replied the kinkajou.

"I won't. I won't. I give you my solemn promise," whined the leopard.

The kinkajou made no answer, and the leopard went on promising, and protesting, until the kinkajou, who was a kind-hearted little creature, decided that he would help. First of all he proceeded to dig deep holes all round the leopard.

"What are you doing now? Why are you wasting time?" groaned the leopard.

"I'm making a lot of holes so that I can escape down one the moment I free you. I don't trust you," replied the kinkajou.

The leopard moaned more protests, false protests, for all the time he was becoming more and more hungry and the kinkajou would be a tasty mouthful.

When all the escape holes were prepared the kinkajou proceeded to gnaw the leopard's bonds. It took a long time, while the leopard watched cautiously, and prepared to spring. At last the bonds fell apart, and all in one movement the leopard sprang free, and leapt towards the kinkajou. But the little animal was too quick for him, and escaped, but not before the leopard had left the marks of his four claws on the poor kinkajou's back. As the kinkajou rushed down the tunnel he resolved never to trust anyone again, and to tell his children never to do so. From that day to this all his descendants never have trusted anyone, not even the kindest human being, and they all bear four marks on their back, like the marks of a leopard's claws.

The leopard went straight to the drinking pool, and after that he went to look for the cunning tortoise, but he never found him, for the tortoise heard what happened, and went off to join his relatives on the Niger. And the kinkajou told everyone how the leopard had tried to kill him, and all the animals shunned the leopard harder than ever. Since then the leopard has no friends.

THE MAN WHO WAS TOO CLEVER

THERE WAS ONCE a boy named Lobo who was so clever, that people declared him to be the cleverest boy they had ever known. From the earliest age he seemed able to learn everything twice as fast as everyone else, and to do it with very little trouble. He had many brothers and sisters, but they were not particularly clever, and it soon came about that he was treated like some very special person, much superior to other people.

Lobo's family were not wealthy, and they all worked hard on their farm, and hunted in their spare time. Lobo didn't care overmuch for hunting. He preferred to set traps. He did this so cleverly that the family were seldom short of meat, which they also shared with their neighbours. Now animals that can be eaten are known as game, and as the years passed Lobo set so many traps in the neighbourhood that game became quite scarce.

A wise old man pointed this out to Lobo. "Ours is not a good country for game, and unless we do less trapping, and make shift with occasional meat, we shall find ourselves with none in a few years' time. I've seen it happen before!"

Lobo looked at the old man contemptuously. He reckoned there would be enough game for years to come, and he wasn't a person who looked very far ahead, or cared much what happened to others. So he simply went ahead and continued to lay traps.

The rest of the time he made elaborate plans. Some had to do with ways of making work easier, some were connected with the future. It was soon clear, however, that most of Lobo's labour saving ideas were of great benefit to himself. More and more of his time was spent in advising other people how to do things, and less and less in doing anything himself. Nevertheless, between one thing and another Lobo prospered, and his family prospered along with him, and when the time came he married the daughter of a Chief. After that he did less work than ever, because Chiefs have to hold many Councils, and Lobo was always present on such occasions.

All the same Lobo was not altogether popular. "He's too clever," some people said. What they really meant was that he was selfish, and indeed he was.

With the passing of the years the scarcity of game increased just as the wise old man had predicted, and not even Lobo's traps were of much use. It was quite an event for the village to have meat. When they did get it, it was as often as not a gift from a white man who had come to live in the district and who had guns. This man's job was to look after the forest, and the game, and he explained to the villagers that he didn't want to shoot more game than he could help for fear the animals would disappear altogether.

Lobo of course had no patience with such ideas. If only he could have got possession of a gun himself he would have shot all the animals he could find, but he couldn't obtain a gun, and he was afraid to steal one because the theft would have been traced.

One day Lobo was wandering through the bush looking at his empty traps when he met an evil old man who practised black magic. Now this old man was very fond of meat, and like Lobo he bewailed the fact that it was so scarce.

Lobo got into conversation with him, and made many bitter complaints about the empty traps.

"The only person who can get game is the white man because he has guns. If I had a gun I could get it also."

"And what does the white man do with the game?" asked the magician.

"If it's very small game he eats it himself, if it's anything bigger he shares it out, and the share is so small it isn't worth taking as a rule," Lobo growled.

"It would be all right if you got the whole of it, say just for yourself, and a friend," suggested the Magician.

"It certainly would," Lobo agreed, "but there's no chance of that. The white man is a stupid fellow. He is fool enough to think everyone should share alike."

"I see," said the Magician. "What if his game disappeared after he shot it?"

"No human being could get near his camp, it's too well guarded," Lobo replied. "As a matter of fact I investigated that aspect of the matter long ago."

"But an animal might get in!" the Magician suggested.

"What do you mean?" Lobo asked curiously.

"If someone were willing to be turned into an animal, say a hyena, they could steal the meat quite easily. It would be a simple job for a clever fellow," and the Magician eyed Lobo shrewdly.

"Meaning who?" enquired Lobo.

"You—if you aren't afraid," said the Magician.

"You mean you could turn me into a hyena?" exclaimed Lobo.

"I could. All I ask is that you share half the meat with me."

"Certainly," said Lobo, highly delighted. "But are you quite sure you can turn me into a hyena?"

"I can. Next time the white man makes a kill you come to me at dusk, and I'll turn you into a hyena. Then you can creep into his camp when it's dark, steal the meat, bring it to me, and after that I'll turn you back into a man again."

Although rather scared Lobo was fascinated at the notion. Few people would have had the courage to submit to such an ordeal, he told himself. But he wasn't like the others, he had brains.

"I agree," he told the Magician. "Next time the white man makes a kill, I'll come to you. Where shall I find you?"

"About half a mile from here you will see a very thick thorny stretch of bush. It looks as if it was a solid mass of trees and scrub, but in the centre there is a small clearing, and I have a hut there."

"Splendid," Lobo said admiringly, and bade the Magician farewell.

A couple of days later Lobo heard that the white man had shot a large buck, and that next day he was going to share it out. So at sunset Lobo hurried off to the Magician. He soon found the particular stretch of bush the old creature had described, and it was indeed an extraordinarily good hide-out. If Lobo had not had very sharp eyes he would never have found the track that led into the centre, it was like walking between solid walls of bush.

The Magician was tending a fire over which a pot smoked and bubbled.

"I heard you coming so I made preparations," he explained. "Sit down for a while." Lobo did as he was bid, and soon the Magician ladled a foul smelling brew out of the pot, and presented it to Lobo. "Now swallow it," he commanded, and began to mutter strange incantations. Obediently Lobo swallowed the stuff, and almost at once he felt strange changes taking place in his body. He shut his eyes tightly and tried not to cry out. A moment later the strange

feelings departed, and he opened his eyes to find he was a nasty looking furry creature, rather like a mixture of wolf and mongrel dog. In
fact he was a hyena, that despised scavenger of the animal world.

Lobo screwed round to have a look at himself.

"Well, I'm not much to look at," he commented. "But I
suppose I'll be able to do the job."

"You certainly will. You had better set off now, and wander
round a bit just to get used to yourself," advised the Magician.

So Lobo set off, and as soon as he became accustomed to the
sensation of walking on four legs instead of two he began to find
the experience very interesting. All sorts of small nocturnal animals
were creeping about, but they took no notice of Lobo. Hyenas
never hunt, they only steal meat already killed by other animals,
and the animals know this and are not afraid of them. This was
very reassuring until Lobo remembered that some of the larger
animals did kill hyena. After that he proceeded with the utmost
caution, and made for the main highway as soon as he could.

He then decided it would be fun to wander round the village.
This he proceeded to do, slipping cleverly from shadow to shadow
so that he was unobserved. Unfortunately the old adage that listeners
never hear good of themselves proved only too true because he had
not gone very far before he heard two of the villagers discussing him.

"Where is Lobo this evening?" asked one.

"Oh probably away by himself somewhere thinking out some
wonderful plan to make more work for us, and less for himself."

"Come now," said the other. "You must admit most of his ideas
are good?"

"Yes, but mostly good for Lobo. No one else gets much out of
them!"

"Perhaps so, but all the same he's a clever fellow."

"Too clever if you ask me."

Lobo was so annoyed he snarled with irritation.

"Whatever was that?" exclaimed one of the men.

"Oh only some nasty hyena hanging around to see if he can steal
something," replied the second, and picking up a stone threw it
with such accuracy that it hit Lobo on the ear, much to his fury,
but there was nothing he could do but lope off into the bush. After
that he made his way slowly, and cautiously to the white man's
camp where he proceeded to spy out the land.

The tents had been surrounded by a thick circle of thorn which
no man could have penetrated, but which a hyena could slip

through. The embers of the fire were dying, but as Lobo watched
the boys proceeded to pile branches on it, and then they lay down
round it and settled themselves for the night.

Shortly afterwards the light in the other tent went out and the
white man settled down to sleep. Lobo waited for a bit longer,
then he slipped silently under the thorn hedge, lying flat in order
to do so, and made his way like a shadow to the kitchen quarters.
There hung a fine buck. Lobo crawled up on to the roof, loosened
the buck from its hook, and it slipped to the ground. The thud it
made was not very loud, and it awakened nobody. Then slowly
and cautiously Lobo began the really difficult task of dragging the
buck towards the hedge as quietly as possible. It had to be done
very slowly so as to make no noise, and Lobo complimented himself on his nerve. One incautious tug might have ruined everything. Fortunately it was a dark night, and Lobo ran little fear of
detection so long as he made no sound. When he actually got the
carcass to the edge of the thorn bushes it was of course more difficult, and some noise was unavoidable, but by wriggling through
himself and dragging the buck slowly after him he made little
sound, and didn't wake anyone. Once outside he was more daring,
and when he got out of earshot he made up for lost time. By midnight he had reached the Magician's hut, tired, hot and hungry.

The Magician was delighted to see him; in an instant he was
changed into a man again, and they proceeded to skin and cook the
buck over a huge fire. Then they had an enormous meal, and for
many nights afterwards they supped off the remains of the buck.

The news of the theft spread round the village next morning.
The white man and his servants were most upset. They had seen
the footprints of an animal, and realised that some four-footed thief
had stolen the buck. The villagers were terribly disappointed
because they would have no meat, and the white man promised
that next time he would see that the meat was not stolen.

But during the weeks that followed the thefts continued. Lobo
devised all sorts of ways of defeating the precautions taken by the
white man. It became a thrilling game to pit his wits against everyone else. He believed he was quite entitled to take the meat if he
was clever enough to secure it, and naturally the Magician backed
him up. His task was made a little easier by the fact that he was
usually able to learn in advance about any precautions that were
taken to protect the meat, because during the day it was quite easy
to talk to the servant boys, and find out exactly what was going on.

By this time the white man was completely puzzled. He could not understand how any animal could be clever enough to get round all the precautions, and avoid all the booby traps laid for him. Finally, the white man began to wonder if some human was behind the thefts. He conceived the idea that perhaps some man had trained a dog to do the job. For this reason the white man decided on stern measures which he mentioned to nobody.

That day he had killed a small deer, and he hung it beside his own tent, and determined that he would sit up all night and watch, gun in hand. Lobo had arrived early to spy out the land, but observed nothing unusual, except that the deer was hung near the white man's bed, but that didn't worry him very much. He was so confident by this time that he would have risked anything. Anything that was, except the real situation which he did not know about. He saw the light go out, but he did not know that the white man had fixed up a dummy in his bed, and was crouching, gun in hand a few feet from where the deer hung.

In blissful ignorance Lobo made his way soundlessly through the thorn bushes, and crept slowly towards the spot where the deer was hanging. He had seized it in his mouth before he saw the movement made by the white man as he raised his gun. There was a flash, Lobo felt a stinging pain in his shoulder, and then he turned and fled. Even then he did not completely lose his presence of mind for he avoided the brighter patches of ground, and ran in the shadows. Also he was clever enough not to make for the spot where he had entered, but to another which he also knew.

Shots rang out behind him as he ran, but once through the hedge he was safely in the bush, and no one could have caught him. This was just as well for his shoulder was hurting badly, and he limped painfully back to the Magician to tell the story of failure for the first time.

The Magician was very alarmed when he heard what had happened, which of course he was unable to learn until he had changed Lobo back into a man. "This is a very serious situation," he told Lobo. "If it were known I should be exiled for my part in it!" "But what of me!" exclaimed Lobo. "The people would be so angry they might kill me!" "That is true," agreed the Magician. "It seems to me there is only one thing to do!" "What is that?" asked Lobo. "I'll tell you in a minute," said the Magician, "Here drink this, and you'll feel better!" He handed Lobo a cup, and Lobo drank. In a moment he had turned into a hyena again. Amazed and indignant he made protesting noises. "There was nothing else I could do," the Magician told him. "You could never have explained away that bullet wound even if I had kept you here, and succeeded in healing you. As a hyena you will recover much more quickly and easily, and no one will seek to kill you provided you keep away from the white man. Also you will be unable to talk, which is very advisable, both from your point of view and mine!"

Snarling and snapping Lobo tried to attack the Magician, but his shoulder was too painful for him to do anything, so he sat down and sulked.

"Calm yourself," said the Magician. "You will find life as a hyena has its good points. If you scavenge cleverly you will get your share of all the meat that is going, and you won't have to do any work. Now let me tend your wound!" So the Magician tended Lobo's wound, and after that they both slept until long after the sun rose.

They were awakened by the sound of people forcing their way through the bushes, and before they could move the white man broke into the clearing.

"See," he cried. "I was right. I knew all along it was some sort of trained animal that was stealing the meat. His blood has led us straight here to himself—and his owner!"

Before the startled Magician could rise the servants at a command from the white man seized him, but Lobo was too quick for them. He darted under a thorn bush, and was soon wriggling his way to freedom. He reached the path and plunged into the bush on the other side, and didn't pause until his wound forced him to rest.

He had a hard time until his wound healed because he had little to eat, but when he recovered he became a notorious scavenger and thief. On the whole he didn't greatly mind being a hyena. He would have minded a great deal more if people had known about it, but they didn't, and among the hyena tribe he was already regarded as an up-and-coming leader. Because he was completely selfish he didn't miss any of his family or friends.

The Magician had been sent to gaol, and every time Lobo thought about this he laughed. It was a very loud unpleasant laugh, all hyenas laugh very unpleasantly, but Lobo sounded even less pleasant than the others. So if ever you go to Africa and hear a particularly nasty hyena laugh in the wilds at night, it's quite likely to be Lobo thinking about the Magician languishing in gaol.

THE BEES AND THE BUFFALO

ONE OF THE most disagreeable and dangerous animals in the African bush is the buffalo. If he strays near crops or gardens he tramples them down. If he decides someone is an enemy he stalks him most cunningly, and attacks him from behind. If buffalo start wandering about near a village they make a lot of trouble.

Once there was a very powerful family of these animals who became tired of where they were living, so they moved up country to a place where there was forest and river, and villages with large crops. The animals in this district were living very happily, there was no scarcity of food, and life was very pleasant. Tortoise sat on the banks of the river, deer wandered in the forest, and hares nibbled some of the crops, but there was so much that nobody minded. Of course there were dangers as there always are in the bush. Most people kept a wary eye on the snakes, and no one ventured too near the lions, but most of the animals were on very good terms.

Then the buffalo strayed in and trouble began immediately. They trampled on the crops, they stamped on small animals and never even noticed, and they wallowed in the mud on the river bank, and the tortoise family only escaped with their lives because of their thick shells.

Now the buffalo were under the rule of a leader, a big, cunning old fellow who was a regular bully. After they had been there for some time so much damage had been done that the animals held a meeting.

They all sat round, and tried to decide what to do.

The tortoise who was a peaceful fellow suggested that they should talk to the buffalo chief, point out how much damage he and his family had caused, and see if they could be persuaded to be more careful.

So they went in search of the old chief. They found him asleep. "If we wake him he'll be very cross," said the deer. "I think we had better put it off." "Nonsense," said the lion. "After walking all this way we are going to say what we have to say," so he roared, "Buffalo," and the old fellow woke up with a great start.

"What do you mean by waking me?" he snorted, as he eyed the animals angrily. "We are very sorry that we had to awaken you, but we have come from all over the forest in order to talk to you."

"What do you want with me?" grunted the buffalo.

"We wish to ask you to be a little more careful," said the tortoise. "Probably you aren't aware that you have caused us some trouble, quite unintentionally, no doubt." Here the lion snarled because he was in no mood for diplomacy, but the tortoise went on smoothly. "You have walked on a number of birds and small animals, and killed them. You have also walked on myself and members of my family, and we only escaped with our lives because of our thick shells. Worse still you have trodden down the crops on the farms, and man is getting angry, and will come to hunt you out. Once he starts hunting there is no knowing where he will stop, and we shall suffer also. We have come to beg of you to keep away from the crops, to leave some of the river bank for myself and my family, and the turtle family who live there also."

"And to be a bit more careful when you walk," squeaked the hare.

The buffalo lashed his tail angrily.

"I am living as I have always lived. We are the lords of the bush, and we cannot be bothered with all this nonsense from lesser folks. Look after your own affairs, and I'll look after mine, and if man interferes with me so much the worse for him!"

At this the lion became very angry indeed.

"So you think you are the Lord of the Bush," he roared. "You big, stupid bully, why everyone knows that the lions are the Kings of the animal world. Come and prove your foolish boast. Come on and fight!" and with that the lion rushed at the buffalo.

"Please," called the tortoise. "Please, gentlemen, this will never do!"

But he was swept aside, and the two combatants sprang at each other. The other animals formed a large ring, and watched with great anxiety. They knew the lion was getting middle-aged, and he hadn't fought for a long time, and they were very much afraid that he would be defeated.

They soon realised that their worst fears were true. The buffalo seemed quite indifferent to the claws of the lion, although he was badly mauled, but in a little while he had the lion down, and then he broke the lion's back, and the lion died.

The animals were most upset when they saw this. They were not intimate with the lion, but they had known him for years, and they were used to him. The python was more angry than anyone, because secretly, he believed, that he was more powerful than any lion, and that if he had attacked the buffalo he would have won.

The buffalo shook himself and glared around.

"I hope this settles who is lord of this district. Does anyone else want to dispute it?" he roared.

"Yes, I do," hissed the python, and made for the buffalo.

"Dear, dear," squeaked the hare, "this is very serious!" It was very serious because it soon became clear that the python was also getting the worst of things. Unlike the lion, however, the python knew when he was beaten, and he had no intention of fighting to the death. Torn and bleeding, he dragged himself away leaving the buffalo triumphant. The other animals followed the python and helped him home.

"We should never have gone near the fellow. We should have tried other methods," lamented the hare. "For once I agree with you," said the tortoise. "We'll have to rely on brains, not brawn." "What do you mean to do?" asked the deer. "I'll do some thinking," replied the tortoise. "If the hare will stay with me he can take a message later on. I advise all you people to go home, and lie low."

"This is bad, you know," the hare said as the others went away. "I went over to the farms for a little corn this morning, and I heard men threatening to come and hunt out the buffalo, and once they start that no one will be safe till they get him—if they get him."

"With our assistance I think they may," said the tortoise. "Will you go and fetch the Queen Bee here, and also a monkey." So the hare ran off and fetched back the Queen Bee and a monkey.

"Would you do us a great favour, Queen Bee, and give us a hive so that we may catch the buffalo who is causing us so much trouble."

The Queen Bee buzzed. "It's a very great sacrifice to give you a hive, but if you think it will help I suppose I'll have to agree."

"I want you to allow two monkeys to take it away."

"Very well, come in an hour, and you may have it," said the Queen, and away she flew.

"Now would you call the wild pigs, and bring some of them here?" the tortoise asked the hare. So the hare set off to find the wild pigs. As usual they were busy digging, but he persuaded some of them to come along.

"I want you to dig a very big, very deep hole under that tree," the tortoise told them. "What do we get for doing it?" asked a pig. "Nothing, but you get rid of the buffalo if that interests you." "It certainly does," squealed the pig. "All the fungus in this part of the bush will be ruined if that clumsy brute isn't put in his place." "He'll be put in his place all right," the tortoise replied.

So the pigs dug an enormous hole, and then the tortoise asked the monkeys to cover the hole with leaves, and branches. "A trap, a trap," shrieked the monkeys, and set to with a will, because there was nothing they enjoyed more than playing tricks, and a trick that might capture the buffalo was really worth while. They concealed the trap so cunningly that no one could guess it was there.

When it was done the tortoise instructed the monkeys to fetch the beehive, and place it just on the other side of the trap.

When the monkeys had done this also, the tortoise drew one of them aside, and whispered in his ear. The monkey nodded eagerly, his eyes sparkling in anticipation, and then off he went to find the buffalo leader.

He eventually found him wallowing in mud. The monkey sat on the river bank, wept loudly, and shrilly, and rubbed himself with mud.

"What on earth is the matter with you?" thundered the buffalo.

"I have had a most unfortunate accident," sobbed the monkey. "I was helping myself to a little honey this morning, and I accidentally knocked down a hive, and the bees returned and attacked me most cruelly. I'm stung all over, and there is all that beautiful honey and I feel too ill to eat any of it."

"Where is it?" asked the buffalo.

"Under that very big tree just over there," said the monkey. "Oh dear, I think I'll lie down in the mud, and see if that helps!" So the monkey lay down, covered his eyes with his paws, and pretended to be in agony while he watched the buffalo go slowly towards the tree by a very roundabout route.

"Here he comes," squeaked the hare, who had been acting as a scout. "Off with you and wait, he's a very cunning fellow," replied the tortoise.

So they stayed at a safe distance until the buffalo came, very quietly for one of his build, spied the hive, and went towards it. Then there was a most terrific crash and the buffalo landed in the pit. His roars positively shook the ground.

·The hare ran out, and danced for joy.

"We've got him. We've got him," he squeaked.

"We haven't finished the job yet," said the tortoise. "Now you run to the village, and frisk around till the dogs see you, and then when they chase you, you lead them here."

So the hare ran off to the village, and frisked around until a dog saw him. The dog immediately barked, and began to chase the hare, and then all the other dogs in the village joined in, and they all ran after the hare. Of course they had chased him before, and they knew, and the hare knew, that they hadn't the slightest chance of catching him, but still it was good fun. The hare led them straight to the trap where the buffalo was roaring, and when he got there he jumped over the trap, and ran to safety. The dogs, their hair rising with excitement, stood on the edge of the pit and barked madly.

Back in the village the terrible commotion made by the dogs attracted the attention of the men. "What are the dogs up to?" they asked. "Without doubt they have cornered some quarry. Let us go and see," suggested an old man. So the men got together, and made their way into the bush until they came to the place where the buffalo was trapped. When they saw what had happened they cried out for joy. "It's the buffalo who has been tramping down our crops. We shall kill him, and have a big feast!"

So they killed the buffalo and dragged the body away, and made a great fire, and held a magnificent feast. The men ate buffalo, and the dogs ate buffalo, and back in the bush the buffalo family decided that as they had lost their leader they had better find a safer place, so they moved off deeper into the bush, and never came back.

The tortoise and the hare and the monkey congratulated each other heartily, and the snake nursed his wounds, and was well content.

WHY PIGS DIG

YOU MAY NOTICE that pigs, wherever they may be, always seem to spend their spare time digging, and snuffling in the ground, and they go on and on as if they were looking for something. All this began a long time ago in the good old days when all the animals could talk to each other.

There was a turtle who was heavily indebted to a pig, and who was always making excuses for not paying his debts. One day when the pig felt that matters had dragged on for long enough, he announced that he would call at the home of the turtle to collect his money. When the pig arrived he found the place in an uproar with the turtle sitting in front of the house wailing loudly.

"Whatever is the matter, old man?" enquired the simple pig.

"Alas, my poor father has passed away," wept the turtle. "He was a fine old chap, and I am stricken with grief," and the turtle broke into heartbreaking sobs.

The pig felt very compassionate.

"All right," he said. "I won't bother you with business matters now, I shall return tomorrow."

So the pig went home, and told his friends what had happened. By next day, however, some of the pig's natural caution had returned, and he decided that this time he would bring a friend with him as witness to any more excuses.

When they arrived at the turtle's home everything seemed quiet, very quiet indeed. Everyone was sitting around as if they had nothing to do, and nowhere to go.

"I'm glad to find everyone seems calmer today," the pig said to the turtle. "Now perhaps we can talk quietly, and you will see how much you can pay off your debt to me."

The turtle shook his head mournfully.

"I am deeply grieved that I can pay nothing today. After you left yesterday there came news of the death of my mother-in-law, and all the money I had has gone to pay for singers at her funeral. There is nothing left, all we can do is to sit here, and wait and see if things are better tomorrow."

The pig began to feel suspicious about these bereavements, but he decided to give the turtle another chance. "Very well," he grunted. "I hope things are better tomorrow, because I shall come back, and I really must insist that some repayment is made to me."

Next day the pig returned, and brought two other pigs with him. Again everything seemed suspiciously quiet, and the turtle began to talk before the pig could say a word.

"My dear fellow," the turtle said, "Believe me I am most anxious to repay you, but this week one thing after another seems to be happening. Yesterday after you had gone I received a reminder that today was my grandmother's centenary, and all the money and food I had, has been taken away for a feast. It is, of course, a most important function, and custom demands that I should give everything I have. I should be at the celebration now, but I waited until you came in order to explain matters to you. We must have another meeting soon, but I must get away now."

"Then I shall return tomorrow," squealed the pig, now thoroughly enraged, and he turned tail, followed by his two friends, and stamped off.

The turtle was now in an awful fix. His excuses were outworn, but he loathed the idea of paying his debts. At last he thought of a scheme to put things off for some time.

"You must pretend to be a doctor," he told his eldest son, "And you will say that after all the troubles I have had lately I became very ill, and that you have ordered me away for a change, and that it's no use the pig coming here day after day as I won't be here."

"And where will you be?" asked the son.

"I shall be here, of course, but the pig mustn't know. Just before he comes tomorrow, you can turn me upside down, spread herbs over me, and pretend I'm a grinding stone. Then the pig and his friends may search all over the place. They won't find me, and they'll go away."

"I don't like this trickery," the son said. "You'll have to pay him something sooner or later."

"Then it will be later—much later," snapped the turtle.

So when the pig arrived he found all the turtle's relatives working around the place, and the youngest son was apparently grinding herbs on an old grinding stone. He saw no sign of the turtle.

"Where is your father?" he demanded of the youngest boy.

"There is a message for you," mumbled the youngster.

At this the eldest son came out, informed the pig—who had brought three friends with him this time—that the turtle was ill from grief and had been sent away for a change of air.

While he told this tale, the youngest son, who found it impossible to remain calm, and pretend to grind the herbs, moved back into the house, leaving the "grinding stone" unattended in front of the pig, but the wily turtle didn't move. He was quite sure his disguise was complete protection, and he remained quite still and listened to his eldest son telling the story as planned.

"And when will the turtle be back?" enquired the pig, almost suffocating with rage at the end of the tale.

"I'm sure I can't tell you," replied the "doctor" smoothly.

Beside himself with anger the pig rushed at the first thing he saw which happened to be the "grinding stone," picked it up and threw it into the bush. Then he sat down.

"I shall stay here till he returns, and so will my friends," he snorted. "These excuses have gone on long enough. The turtle must take me for a complete fool!"

Meanwhile the turtle picked himself up out of the bush, and crept into the house by the back door. His youngest son was terrified. "Don't be alarmed," said the turtle. "I see a way out of this at last. Call your brother in."

When the eldest son came in the turtle whispered that he now had a plan which was going to settle matters, and they were to follow his lead, and back him up in everything he said. Then he crept out through the bush, made his way to the road, and with as much noise as possible, calling out as he came, he moved towards the front of the house.

"Why it's my father," exclaimed the eldest son. "He has come back."

"Now what is he up to?" grunted the pig.

"I had to return," announced the turtle. "I was so ill last night I forgot all about my appointment with you," he told the pig. "But this morning I remembered it and I came back. I feel I must do something to repay you."

"Good," replied the pig. "Give me what you owe me, and let me go, that's all I ask."

"Yes," said the turtle. "Yes, I shall call my sons, and we shall see what we can arrange. What have you been doing this morning? I hope you have entertained the Doctor properly. Did you grind the herbs, and make him a meal?" he asked the youngest son.

"I was grinding the herbs when the pig came," said the youngest son.

"Let me see if they are properly ground, where is the grinding stone?" asked the turtle.

"Well, the pig got rather annoyed, and threw it into the bush," said the youngest son.

"Fetch it at once," demanded the turtle.

"I'll fetch it," said the pig, feeling a bit of a fool. So off he trotted into the bush and went to the spot where he judged the grinding stone to have fallen. Of course it was not there.

"Have you found the grinding stone?" called the turtle.

"No," replied the pig. "It must have rolled away."

The turtle set up a wail.

"Oh dear, and it's a most valuable stone. It was my grandfather's, it's been in the family for hundreds of years. It's priceless. Please find it at once."

"We'll help you," cried the pig's friends, and they went, and rooted round in the bush as well, but of course there was no grinding stone to be found. All the while they searched the turtle became more and more anguished. "It has fallen into a deep hole, or it has been stolen," he wailed.

The pigs continued to search frantically, but after a time they had to give up, and they went back to the turtle feeling very guilty.

The turtle was sitting in front of his house, weeping, and quite beside himself.

"Look what has happened now," he cried, "and all over that silly debt that I could have paid in no time, now you have lost my precious grinding stone which was worth a hundred times as much as my debt to you. It must be found. I don't care how far you search or how long it takes, but you must find my grinding stone. I refuse to repay anything until it is found."

The poor pig realised he was in a hopeless position unless he found the grinding stone, so he decided to call out all his friends to help in the search, and to send out messages to all pigs everywhere to find the lost or stolen grinding stone. Then he went back to snuffling and digging himself. By next day all the pigs in the bush were hard at the task, and as appeals went out more and more pigs joined in the search. Needless to say they have been searching ever since, all over the world, but they have never found the grinding stone.

THE LAME AND THE BLIND

IN A VILLAGE there were two men who met with great misfortune. One of them began to get a cataract over his eyes and to grow blind. The other had a severe fever, and it was a long time before he recovered. When he did recover he found that he was lame. Instead of being able to walk, and run about and tend his farm he had to sit down and watch others, so he found himself in the company of the blind man, who also had to remain idle.

"Ah, if only I had your legs," mourned the lame man. "I could go and work on my farm. Now I feel as useless as a log."

"And if only I had your eyes," complained the blind man, "then I could make use of my legs."

This gave the lame man an idea.

"You are a fine, big, strapping fellow, and I am small. If you will carry me on your back, I'll tell you which way to go, and we need not sit idly here," he suggested.

"That wouldn't be easy," said the blind man.

"I know it wouldn't, but it's worth trying!" So the lame man climbed on the blind man's back.

"Now set out, I'll be your eyes, and you can be my legs!"

So off they went. At first it was a slow and clumsy business, because the blind man tripped over small obstacles, but they went on trying, and after some weeks they got around splendidly, and went off and tended their farms, and did not have to sit idle any more.

As time passed there was little they could not do, and they even became a little jealous of each other, each trying to outdo the other in some small feat.

"Let us kill a chicken for dinner," the lame man suggested one day.

"However shall we manage to do that?" asked the blind man.

"You do exactly as I say, and we'll manage it. When I say 'Run,' don't be afraid to run."

"All right," agreed the blind man, "but I don't like it."

So they proceeded to run after the chicken, and after a strenuous chase they caught it.

"Now you sit down," said the lame man. "I'll prepare the chicken, and we'll have a real feast."

As the lame man prepared the chicken he began to think that it would be a great pity if he had to share it with the blind man. He thought very hard about how he could manage to keep it all for himself. As he was washing the chicken in the stream he saw a very large frog sitting on the bank. Edging forward he suddenly threw himself on the startled frog, and killed it. Then he proceeded to prepare it for cooking along with the chicken. He knew some frogs were tender, and he hoped this one was.

Then he began to wonder if the flavour would give the game away so he put a great deal of spice, and pepper into the pot.

When the chicken was cooked he judged that the frog must be cooked also, so he took them out, and put them on a large dish which he took along to the blind man.

"What a long time you have been," the blind man complained, when he heard his companion crawling along.

"I cooked the chicken in a very special way, I'm sure it's going to taste different to any chicken you ever ate before," said the the lame man, and putting down the dish, he carefully turned the side with the frog towards his companion.

"I seem to have the whole bird," the blind man said as he groped round the frog.

"I want you to have the best of it, just pull off a little bit for me," the lame man replied.

So the blind man picked up the frog, and tried to tear it in halves, but the frog was very tough, and gave him great trouble.

"You certainly have cooked this in a very special way, it's so tough I can't tear it apart," the blind man said angrily.

"It must have been a tough old bird," replied the lame man. "Give it a good hard pull; you'll find it will be delicious once you do get it apart."

So the blind man gave a mighty heave, and the frog flew in halves, and the pepper with which it was coated flew into the blind man's eyes. The blind man danced, and howled, and wept and blinked, and then to his great surprise he suddenly found he could see once more.

The first thing he saw was what he held in his hands, and it was quite evident it was not a chicken. His face became convulsed with rage, and the lame man realised that unless he could escape he was in for a good beating. He was so terrified that he began to run, not realising the amazing fact that he had regained the use of his legs.

So the lame man ran, and the blind man pursued him right through the village, and out into the open country until they encountered a farmer returning from work. He was a great big burly man, so the lame man ran and hid behind him.

"Save me, save me," he cried. "I'm a poor cripple, and the blind man will kill me."

The farmer looked at the pair, and decided that the first one must be mad.

"What are you talking about?" he asked. "How can you be a cripple, when you are running like the wind, and how can this fellow be blind when he is running after you?"

So they both began to talk at once until the bewildered farmer had grasped the truth of their story.

"This man is violent, he's a dangerous fellow," ended the lame man. "Our chicken must now be eaten by the dogs."

"And this fellow is a cheat and a villain," yelled the blind man. "He tried to fob me off with a frog for my dinner."

The farmer began to roar with laughter.

"Well I think you must both be mad. You've got back the use of your legs," he told the lame man, "and you've got back your sight," he reminded the blind man, "and all you can do is to squabble over a silly chicken and a frog."

At this the two men quietened down and looked sheepish.

"You're right," said the lame man, "we are very silly people. And I apologise for trying to cheat *you* over the chicken, my old friend, it's because I was so jealous that you had good legs, and I was lame—or at least I thought I was."

"I quite understand," the blind man responded. "Anyhow, it was all for the best."

So the two of them patched up their quarrel, and turned and hurried back to the village to tell everyone of the wonderful thing that had happened to them.

Which proves that disappointments are often blessings in disguise.

BUSH BABY

THERE WAS A time in Africa when the country was torn by war, and when it was the custom that the victor took away large numbers of the vanquished people to be his slaves. No one was safe, men, women, and even little children, were taken from their homes, formed into gangs, and made to walk through the bush for miles and miles, until they came to the victor's country. There they had to work hard for long hours, and could be bought or sold, or traded for goods.

There was a little boy named Abu whose mother lived in constant dread of war and slave raids. When she was a little girl her parents had been stolen in such a raid, and she had only escaped by hiding in the bush. She was determined that this fate should not overtake her little son, and she told him many times what he must do if strange, fierce men appeared in the village. He was to take to the bush, and hide for a long time, and not come out of hiding until he was quite sure that the slavers had gone.

Abu was very sad when his mother talked of these things, but most of the time he was very gay and happy, because life was pleasant and carefree. Most days his mother took him with her when she went to work on their farm where they grew food. Abu loved the early morning walk to their particular patch of land, and even more he loved returning home in the evening when the fires were lighted, and everyone had a meal, and then sat round and told stories.

The only thing that really scared Abu was the witch who lived some distance from the village. She was a bent and wrinkled old hag whom the villagers visited when there was sickness, or drought, or any other misfortune, and she was reputed to make magic remedies, and to obtain favours from the gods. Abu's mother tried to

117

calm his fears. "She is a wise woman, and must be respected," she told him. "But isn't she wicked and cruel?" Abu asked. "I have heard that she changes people into animals if they displease her." "Then be careful not to displease her," the mother replied.

However Abu was taking no chances. He never went near the house of the witch, and if he saw her coming he ran away, and hid, for she was terrifying in her strange garments, and her bracelets of monkey fur.

Then came rumours of war in the district. Many men went away to fight (among them Abu's father), and by and by came news that they had been defeated, that Abu's father was dead, and that the victorious armies were marching upon the villages.

To make sure her son was safe, Abu's mother hid with him in the bush near their farm, and never left him except to gather food. "If I don't come back don't try to follow me," she said when she left him each morning. For many days this went on, and always after a few hours the mother came back to her son. But one day she did not come back. Abu waited all day till the sun went down, and then lonely and frightened of the dark he made his way cautiously to the village.

A dozen times, as he crept through the bush, he felt sure he was being followed, but he found that it was only animals, and birds, moving around uneasily because of all the strange sights, and sounds that had made that day so unlike other days.

Abu met no strangers, and as he drew near the village he saw the light of the evening fires, and heard men singing. Heartened he hurried forward thinking that nothing much could be wrong after all, but when he drew near he saw a terrible sight. Nearly all the people of the village were crouching on the ground in chains while their captors laughed, danced, and made merry in the fire-light. Anxiously Abu looked for his mother, and then he saw her, one of the crowd of captives. Forgetting all her warnings he cried out, and the men round the fire turned and saw him.

"Run, Abu, run into the bush!" cried the mother, and as the men started towards him, Abu turned, and ran. He slipped through bushes, and around tall trees, slid down deep gullies, and hid under river banks. Now the pursuers were far away, now they were near. On and on Abu struggled. At last in the distance, he saw a light, and made towards it. It was a small, mean house, but to Abu it meant shelter, protection. Without pausing to knock, he opened the door, and darted into the dim interior. The moment he had done so he realised this was no ordinary house, the walls were hung with strange objects, and a small, smoky fire burned in the room. The figure that rose to greet him was clad in curious robes, and had a wizened face like a monkey. It was the witch's house.

Bad as this was, at least Abu knew the witch, and he did not know the strangers who pursued him. "Hide me, hide me!" he gasped. "The slavers are after me!" Without saying a word the witch flung a skin over him, and sat so that she hid his small bulk. Then the men dashed in.

When they saw the witch they paused in dismay, for they were just as much afraid of her as Abu was.

"What is this? Why do you come to my house?" the witch asked in her strange, harsh voice. "We are seeking a boy, he ran this way!" quavered the leader. "Go about your business," said the witch. "Those who enter this house do it at their peril!" The men muttered among themselves, and then withdrew. The witch hobbled across to a small hole in the wall, and watched and listened for some minutes.

"You may come out," she told Abu at last. "They have gone further into the bush."

"But they will come back," Abu said sadly as he threw the skin aside.

"True, but they will not come here. What are you going to do?" Abu sighed.

"I do not know. My father has been killed in the wars, and my mother is captured. I must try and follow them when they take her away, or else I shall not know where she has gone, and will never see her again."

"How do you hope to follow the slave gang without being captured, or else starved or left behind?"

"I don't know," Abu said unhappily. Then he thought over some of the things he had heard about the witch, and almost quivering with fright at his own idea, he made a suggestion.

"Couldn't you help me? I have heard that you can change people into animals. Please change me into something else, and then I can follow my mother."

The witch looked at him curiously.

"Aren't you afraid?" she asked.

"How can things be much worse?" Abu asked.

"I suppose not," replied the witch. "What sort of animal do you want to be?"

Abu looked thoughtful, it was very difficult.

"I can't be a crocodile because I couldn't follow them over the land. If I'm a lion they might kill me, and in any case a lion would frighten my mother. If I'm a giraffe I'll be too remarkable. If I'm a deer I'll probably be attacked and killed by the lions. If I'm a nasty looking animal like a bush pig I'll frighten my mother just as much as if I'm a lion. Oh dear, it is difficult."

"I would advise you to be something small and unremarkable but at the same time quite pretty so you won't frighten your mother when she finds out it's you. I would also suggest that you become a nocturnal animal, that is one that sleeps a lot in day time, and travels at night because that is what the slavers are likely to do."

"That seems a good idea," Abu agreed. "But what shall I be?"

"I think you'd better be a bush baby. They are very small, no bigger than a squirrel, they travel through the tree tops or run over the ground with equal ease, and no one notices them. You will be quite safe."

Abu clapped his hands with joy.

"Oh, thank you so much!" he cried.

The witch grunted.

"You sit down and keep quiet. I have much to do!"

Abu watched round-eyed while the witch made strange, and mysterious preparations. She placed a huge pot on the fire, and proceeded to throw into it a lot of peculiar looking, and vile smelling, substances. Soon there was much steam and smoke in the air and the witch began muttering incantations that made Abu quake with terror.

Then the witch fell silent, poured some of the brew into a cup, and handed it to Abu.

"Drink!" she commanded.

As he was about to raise the cup to his lips Abu was struck by an alarming thought.

"I forgot," he gasped. "I don't want to be a bush baby for ever. You will change me back again, won't you?"

"You come back to me when you want to resume your normal form, and I'll change you back," replied the witch.

Looking into her wicked, laughing eyes, Abu felt sick with doubt. Could he trust her? He did not know. He would have to take the risk.

Abu raised the cup to his lips. It was very bitter, but he drained it to the dregs.

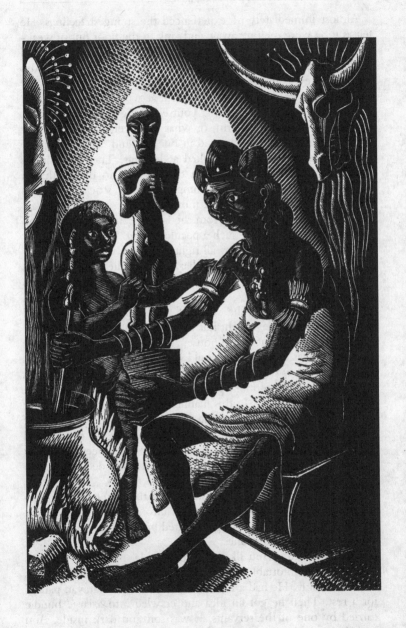

Almost immediately he experienced the strangest feelings. He felt as if he were melting away, and sank to the floor out of weakness and fright. For a moment everything whirled round him, and he gave himself up for dead. Then the whirling stopped, Abu opened his eyes, and saw the witch towering above him.

"How you've grown," he quavered, at which the old woman gave a horrible cackle. "Look at yourself!" she croaked.

Abu stretched out his arm, or what had been his arm, now it was a delicate little paw covered in fine fur, and ending in queer claw like fingers. Then he looked at his legs. They had almost disappeared. He found he was a tiny animal no bigger than a squirrel. For a moment he felt completely panic stricken, then he moved cautiously, and the next moment he had run up the wall, and was hanging suspended from the ceiling, although he had no notion why he had done such a peculiar thing.

"Well, you're a bush baby all right," said the witch.

"I'm certainly something peculiar," Abu replied and found his voice had turned to a high, shrill squeak, but the witch seemed to understand him.

"Now go quickly," she said, "if those men come back and suspect anything, they might kill you!"

Abu scampered out of the house, and was surprised to find that although it was very dark he could see quite well. Also it was fun to travel in a new way, because instead of running over the ground he found himself running up and down trees and swinging from one branch to another. In this manner he reached the village very quickly. It was quiet now. The captors, with the exception of some guards were sleeping, and the captives lay on the ground where he had last seen them, doing their best to sleep also. Abu wondered if he should go to his mother, but deemed it too dangerous. It was better to watch and wait.

Before dawn the village was astir, and in the grey light of morning the poor captives were marshalled into a long row, and were marched off, leaving the village deserted but for a few old people, who wept for their lost ones.

As the sun rose Abu liked the journey less, and less. He was much more comfortable in the dark than in daylight, and his eyes blinked weakly. He had a miserable time until the caravan paused for a rest. Then he got an idea and crawled into a large bundle carried by one of the servants. It was soft and dark inside. Abu curled up comfortably, and slept away the long hours of daylight.

When he awoke he realised that the caravan must have slept during most of the day also, for it was night, and they were marching on. This made it impossible to approach his mother. For four days and nights this programme was repeated. The train marched at night, slept by day, and it was never possible for Abu to go to his mother. He was glad to see however, that the young, strong captives, and his mother was one, had a better time than the weaker, or older people. If these tired, or fell, they were beaten, and when they could walk no longer they were left behind.

Then on the eve of the fourth day Abu realised they were nearing a town. People came out to meet them, and the victorious army was welcomed home. There was also much rejoicing because they had brought so many slaves. The slaves were marched into a large compound, and for the first time their chains were removed, and they were sorted out and shifted into huts. Abu watched anxiously until he saw where his mother was taken, and then he slipped into the hut after her, and crouched in a corner until the poor slaves fell asleep. Then he crept across to his mother, put his paws on her arm, and squeaked.

He had not reckoned on the result, because she thought it was a rat, woke up in terror, and shook him off, staring at him with frightened eyes. Abu sat down and tears rolled down his cheeks. Were all his efforts in vain? Would his mother never realise who he was? "Shoo," she gasped, and poor Abu turned and fled. He ran out of the compound and into the bush. Sitting on the branch of a tree he began to cry pitifully. Because of his shrill voice it sounded like the cry of a baby.

"What is the matter?" squeaked a voice, very like his own.

Abu looked up to discover another bush baby peering at him inquisitively.

Abu poured out his sad story. At first the other bush baby looked as if he didn't believe a word. "You mean you are really a human boy?" he asked. "I am!" "You've been dreaming," scoffed the bush baby. "I have not," Abu squeaked indignantly. "I was born six years ago, and my father was killed in the war, and my mother is in that slave camp, and she's wearing a pink robe with yellow flowers on it, and her name is Daughter of the Blacksmith." The bush baby backed away in alarm. "Ooo, I believe you are telling the truth!" he shrilled.

"Please don't go, don't leave me," Abu sobbed. "My mother was afraid of me because I'm an animal, and now you're afraid of me because I'm really a boy." The bush baby sat down at a safe distance. "Now tell me all about it right from the beginning, and go slowly!" he commanded.

When Abu finished the bush baby flicked his nose nervously, and peered at Abu out of his strange light eyes. "Well, I suppose you are telling me the truth, but it's amazing, and you do seem to be in a mess. What are you going to do?"

"Well, I thought you might help me," Abu suggested.

The little animal jumped.

"Me! How can I help you?"

"Are there many of you in this part of the bush?" Abu asked.

"Not near here, but scattered around there are thousands of us, I expect."

"Then listen," said Abu and proceeded to outline his plan.

The bush baby was at first thoroughly alarmed, but at heart he was kind, and Abu at last persuaded him to try and put the plan into action.

"I'll do my best," he promised at last, "but it will take at least a week to arrange!" With that he departed, and Abu had to settle down to a tiresome wait. In the meanwhile he did not try to get near his mother again. It was both dangerous and useless.

On the sixth night the bush baby returned.

"The plan is arranged," he told Abu. "There are thousands of us waiting. It will be amusing to be the hunters instead of the hunted."

Half an hour later one of the sentries in the compound rubbed his eyes, and decided he must be having a nightmare. Small animals were pouring over the walls and through the gates. They passed over the sentry like a wave, leaving him lying on the ground shivering with fear. They poured into the huts occupied by the captives, who awoke screaming with terror, and scattered in all directions. The sentries were no less frightened, and could do nothing. Abu's mother ran out pursued by hundreds of the little animals. She thought it was that they must have her marked down for destruction, because although she ran till she was breathless they still pursued her, led by one little fellow who seemed forever at her heels.

At last she could run no longer, and sank to the ground behind a bush, closed her eyes, and waited for the end. Nothing happened. When she opened her eyes again there was not an animal to be seen. Gathering her wits together she realised that she was some distance along the trail which she had travelled with the slave caravan, so she crawled into the bush and slept.

She woke at dawn, and it was only then that the real situation struck her dulled mind. She had escaped. She rose to her feet, and avoiding the road, went as fast as she could by small trails through the bush. After she had gone a short distance she heard a rustling behind her, and turned in terror. It was a bush baby, and she recognised him as the same one who had led the invaders the night before. She gathered up her skirts and ran, but was halted by what appeared to be the unhappy cry of a baby. She turned quickly. The little animal was sitting in the middle of the path weeping pitifully. The cry was not to be resisted. Half fearful, the mother turned back, walked towards the little fellow, and put out her hand. To her amazement he crept towards her, snuggled into her hand, and crawled up her shoulder.

"Well, you are a queer little thing," she said. "But you did save me last night. Do you want to come with me?" The bush baby seemed to understand her, for he nodded his head and crept closer still, hiding his weak eyes against the light.

So for that day, and many days after, the mother and the bush baby travelled through the bush until at last they came back to the village. By this time the mother had become attached to the bush baby. "I'll give you to my little son, when I find him," she said. This remark seemed to send the bush baby into a frenzy of emotion, but of course the poor mother had no idea why.

She was therefore very disappointed when she reached the outskirts of the village and the bush baby suddenly scrambled from her shoulder and dashed off as if he had most important business of his own. But when she heard from the villagers that her son had never been seen since her own capture she was too upset to think of the bush baby.

In the meanwhile Abu had rushed to the witch's house, shot through the door, and squeaked wildly at the crone who was crouched over her smoky fire as usual.

"So you've come back. Did you see your mother?"

Squeaking and dancing with impatience Abu told his tale.

"Now change me back, change me back quick!" he implored the witch who was cackling with joy at his recital.

The witch looked at him doubtfully as if trying to make up her mind.

"You promised. You promised!" Abu reminded her. The witch nodded.

"Have patience. Go sit over there and wait!" But Abu couldn't sit except the way bush babies sit, hanging out of the ceiling, which he proceeded to do, watching the witch with anxious eyes.

Again she made strange mixtures that smelled most evilly, and again she eventually produced a brew. This time, however, she had to hold the cup while he licked it up. He had no sooner done so than he felt as if he were swelling up and shooting out in all directions, and again the room seemed to rock round him. Then it steadied, and the witch no longer seemed enormous; she was a small wizened woman again. Abu gazed at himself eagerly. The fur had gone. He was himself once more.

Abu was so relieved and so delighted that he flung his arms round the witch and embraced her. No one had ever done this before and she was so surprised that she stood speechless while he darted out of the hut.

He ran all the way back to the village where he found his mother weeping outside the door of their home. She was overjoyed to see him, and so were all the people left in the village.

From the edge of the bush, as darkness fell, the bush babies, many of whom had taken part in the rescue watched the scene. They were very pleased with themselves about the rescue, for it really was the most important thing they had ever done in their lives, and they felt a glow of pride about it for the rest of their days. Also they had acquired a new trick. They cried like babies as they had heard Abu cry when he was one of them. From that day to this they have retained that cry. So if ever you go through the bush at dark, and hear what appears to be a baby weeping unhappily, don't worry about it. It is only the bush baby, and he is not really unhappy at all.

THE VICTORIOUS TORTOISE

THE TORTOISE IS a very clever fellow. He has to use his wits to get along in the world because he has neither the strength of the lion nor the speed of the hare. However his cleverness doesn't make him popular with everyone, partly because he is inclined to be a bit conceited about it.

For a long time he had irritated the elephant, until one day the elephant became so annoyed that he lost his temper. "You think you're very smart," he shouted. "But if it came to a fair fight I'd win every time!"

"Do you think so?" sneered the tortoise.

"I know so!" said the elephant, and tore up the trunk of a tree and smashed it like a match stick just to show what he could do.

The tortoise moved away a little, and watched the performance, but he was not very much impressed.

"I think you would find you are mistaken," he said calmly. "However if you like we shall try it."

"You mean you will fight me?" said the elephant.

"Exactly. Just at dawn tomorrow morning, on the bank of the river."

"Why the bank of the river?" the elephant asked suspiciously.

"Because the ground is level there, and because it's near where I live. As you started this, I am at least entitled to choose the spot."

"The river is as good a place as any for the disposal of the body," the elephant agreed.

"I hope yours won't block up the river," the tortoise commented.

The elephant put back his head and trumpeted loudly. He shook with laughter until tears ran down his cheeks.

"Oh, go away, before I die of laughter!" he sobbed at last.

127

The tortoise moved away at his usual slow pace. "You'll laugh on the other side of your face my lad," he vowed. As he walked off he saw smiles on the faces of other animals who had heard his encounter with the elephant, but he treated them with contempt, an expression which a tortoise assumes with great ease as you have probably noticed.

He made his way to the river bank where he found the hippopotamus wallowing comfortably in the mud. Now the hippo is an unsociable fellow. If people let him alone, he lets them alone, but if there is any attempt to provoke him he can be very bad tempered indeed.

"Ugh," snuffled the tortoise. "How can you bear to wallow in all that nasty mud. Such a horrible smell!"

"I like it," the hippo growled. "My family have always taken mud baths."

"I think it's a perfectly filthy habit," said the tortoise.

"No one asked you what you thought!" grunted the hippo. "No one asked you to come here either!"

"I have just as much right to be here as you have," snapped the tortoise.

"Then keep a still tongue in your head," the hippo told him.

"You know, your manners leave much to be desired. What a pity you are such a rough diamond. I really should try to do something about it!"

The hippo rose from the mud with gigantic upheaval.

"Oh, you would, would you," he retorted, his little eyes alight with rage. "I don't think so much of your manners myself. In fact I'd like to give you a lesson or two!"

"Are you threatening me?" asked the tortoise calmly.

"Call it what you like, I'm coming to teach you a lesson," the hippo replied, and started to wade towards the tortoise.

"Stop!" said the tortoise. "I don't believe in any rough and tumble business. If you want a fight we'll have one in a proper manner. I'll meet you here at dawn tomorrow, and then we'll see who is the best man!"

The hippo gave an unpleasant laugh.

"Excellent, nothing would suit me better. It's nice and cool then. Don't forget to come though, will you?"

"I certainly shan't forget," said the tortoise, and went away looking very satisfied, as indeed he might be, for his plot was working out perfectly.

News of the contest between the elephant and the tortoise got around, but no one knew about the arrangement of the second fight, because the hippo was too unsociable to talk to anyone. The tortoise was perfectly well aware of that, it was in fact an essential part of his plot.

Shortly before dawn the tortoise rose from his bed by the river bank, and peered through the mists for the elephant. Right enough he soon saw the elephant lumbering along, followed by a large circle of his friends who had come to see the fight.

The tortoise then looked into the river, and there was the hippo lying in wait. As soon as he heard the noise of the approaching crowd he stood perfectly still, so that it was impossible for anyone to detect him in the mist. That also was just the way the tortoise wanted things, and he moved carefully behind some reeds, and waited, until the elephant reached the bank.

"Ho," the elephant chuckled. "So my brave friend has not arrived. I wonder if he has thought better of it."

Just as the elephant passed the spot where the tortoise was hidden, the tortoise grabbed the tip of the elephant's trunk. The elephant was so surprised and hurt that for a moment he was helpless, and during that critical moment the tortoise swung himself straight out over the river bank towards the hippo. The hippo naturally made a grab at his foe, but in his excitement he caught the elephant's trunk, while the tortoise wriggled free, and dropped into the mud.

With a wild heave the hippo dragged the elephant over the bank and into the water, where the two of them thrashed round wildly, and the crowd unaware of what happened, were amazed at the extraordinary strength of the tortoise, who was actually sitting at a safe distance down river watching the gigantic struggles of the elephant and the hippo, who were badly mauled, and had fought themselves to a standstill before they discovered what had occurred.

Then they dragged themselves to the bank, bruised and exhausted.

"What on earth made you attack me?" asked the elephant.

The hippo tried to explain what had happened, and became very excited, but during lengthy and confused explanations, and while practically everyone, including the onlookers, almost had a fight with everyone else, the elephant and the hippo realised that the tortoise had played a very cunning trick on them.

So they apologised to each other, and parted, after vowing that never again would either of them become involved in any arguments with the wily tortoise. The onlookers came to the same conclusion, and that is why the tortoise is always left severely alone. No other animal ever attacks him, and they are all careful to keep on polite terms with him.

THE AMBITIOUS ANTS

ANTS ARE THE busiest creatures in the world. Every ant has a full time job, with no holidays and no half-days off. Ants like to work, and they don't like much else. The biggest and strongest ants build whole cities for themselves, complete with compartments like deep shelters to which they can retreat if any enemies try to destroy the city above. In these cities there are even big stores where food is kept, and special nurseries for young ants.

If you watch ants at work you will notice that they always work in vast numbers. One or two single ants never do anything alone. If they happen to get separated from the regular army they scuttle about in great distress until they find their way into the crowd again. Once there they get into line like soldiers, and march patiently off about their tasks.

This was not always the way they worked. Once there were two ants who had very big ideas about what they could do. They believed that if they could make a tunnel all the way under the earth they would really be able to span the whole world, and that gradually every other creature would have to obey their orders.

They decided that the best way to start this tunnel was to begin burrowing in opposite directions, and then they would eventually meet at the other end.

So each ant began to burrow, and on and on they went. Of course they didn't realise that it was most unlikely that they could work in such a straight line that they would meet in the end. Day after day, they dug, but there was no sign of their meeting. Finally the first ant began to think something was wrong. He decided that his partner was a very foolish fellow who had somehow taken the wrong turning, so he turned round and marched back. After a long and tiresome journey, down the tunnel he had made, he arrived in the open once more.

Here he found everything as usual. Millions of ants were all scurrying around on their accustomed tasks, each one in an awful hurry—you may have noticed ants always are in an awful hurry—and he had to waylay one to ask for information.

"Have you seen or heard anything of my friend who is making a tunnel round the earth?" he asked a young ant who was carrying a large leaf on his back. "No, I haven't," replied the young ant. "But I did see someone being carried off on a stretcher. It may be your friend!"

Seriously alarmed our ant hurried off to the hospital, and made anxious enquiries, but none of the ants brought in during the past few days were his friend. However, the ant on guard at the door had another piece of news. "I did hear about an ant who was going to tunnel his way round the world, he was brought in badly injured some days ago, and he died."

This upset our ant very much, and he at once scurried to the Registrar of Births and Deaths, where he made enquiries into all the burials of the past few days.

"I don't see your friend's name," the Registrar told him. "What makes you think he's dead?"

"Well he was helping to make a tunnel round the world, and it's a pretty dangerous job."

The Registrar laughed.

"Oh is he one of them? Crazy folk are always getting the idea that they can do that, just like some think they are Napoleon, or Julius Caesar, but most of them end up in the Mental Hospital. I should go and look there if I were you!"

Our ant retreated in a thoroughly bad temper, consoling himself with the fact that great men were always misunderstood by those around them. "They said Christopher Columbus was mad too," he muttered, and set off again for his tunnel, determined that he would make an effort to do the job single-handed.

In the meanwhile the second ant had gone on tunnelling, and tunnelling until he was worn out, and still there was no sound of his friend's approach from the other end. So finally he also decided that he would go back and try and find out what was the matter.

After a long, weary journey he emerged into the daylight, and found everyone busy as usual. The only person who took the slightest notice of him was a vulture. As vultures always see everything the ant asked him if his friend had been around.

"Well, I'm not sure if it was him," replied the vulture, "but I did see a fellow calling a meeting yesterday, and it seemed to me that something very queer was going on!" The vulture gave the ant a crafty look. Nothing pleased the vulture better than a fight because the victims always fell to him in the end, so he never missed an opportunity to start some trouble.

"But why should he call a meeting?" asked the ant.

"Well, he might claim that he had circled the earth single-footed, and offer to act as leader to the other ants, and conquer the world at last," suggested the vulture.

"But he couldn't do that, I've done as much as he has!"

"Oh, probably he hasn't done anything of the kind. It's only an idea I had. Forget it," the vulture said cunningly.

The ant went away feeling thoroughly upset. When you put your trust in someone this was always what happened, he told himself, quite forgetting that the vulture hadn't a shred of evidence to support his nasty idea.

"There is only one thing to do," the ant told himself, "I'll have to get people on my side. I'll have to convince them that I am in the right."

So he went into the public square and waved his feelers wildly, but the other ants were as usual so busy marching round on their accustomed tasks that no one took any notice of his antics. Finally, he rolled a large stone into the middle of one of their endless files of marching men, and this broke them up in confusion, and he made them listen to him.

At first they refused to believe that he had really made such a long tunnel as he claimed. They merely tapped their foreheads, and decided that here was someone else who had crazy ideas about conquering the world.

"Give me a fair chance," pleaded the ant. "Come and see what I have done, and then you will believe me!" More in anger than sympathy one of the leaders eventually told off a posse of workers to accompany the ant, and off they went towards the tunnel. Having entered it, and marched, and marched, for miles, they became somewhat impressed, and believed that after all there might be some truth in this amazing claim.

"I know I must be almost all the way round the world," the ant assured them, "and another bit of work will prove it. Come on and help me dig!" So they all helped him, and they dug, and dug until they were weary, and called, and called to try and locate the fellow who was supposed to be digging from the other end, but there was no reply, and finally they were forced to give up.

In the meanwhile the first ant had repeated the performance of his friend. Convinced that he had been betrayed he too called a meeting and recruited a crowd to his aid, and they went back and proceeded to burrow further along his tunnel, but without any result. The only person who was pleased was the vulture, who could see some really worthwhile developments from his personal viewpoint.

After much time had passed both gangs of workers gave up and made their way back along the tunnels until they at last emerged face to face. At once both the leaders advanced on each other furiously, and made accusations of treachery, while the eager vulture sat up on a tree above, almost drooling in anticipation of a huge meal of slaughtered ants.

However, all the ants weren't hot-heads, and as each side listened it became clear to many of them that the whole misunderstanding lay in the original idea that two ants burrowing in opposite directions round the world, could meet on the other side.

So they broke up the argument by pointing this out to the leaders.

"If you ask me," one old ant commented, although no one had asked him anything, "If you ask me, all the trouble arose because you two tried to do this thing on your own. If you had worked with an organised army the way we usually do, everything might have been all right. I think a resolution should be passed that in future, all ants, everywhere, will never work alone, but always in large numbers."

The original leaders had nothing to say against this plan, for they felt more than a little foolish, and so the resolution was passed unanimously. From that day to this no ant ever does anything alone, and if you want to see this for yourselves all you need do is to go into the garden and watch till you see ants at work.

As regards their idea of ruling the world it never came to anything, because quite apart from the difficulties, there aren't enough ants for the job. True there are billions, and billions of them, but that isn't enough.

THE VAIN GIRL

THROUGHOUT ALL AFRICA the crocodile has a great reputation for wisdom, but it doesn't help to make him popular, no one trusts him very much. When someone has done wrong, it is a frequently threatened punishment to "Throw him to the crocodiles!" and in the bad old days this was a very real threat.

Now there was a girl whose name in our language was Jewel, because she was very beautiful. She was the eldest of three sisters, and from the time she was born her beauty was most remarkable, which, as you know is unusual in very young babies, because they are rather plain.

Because of her beauty Jewel was made much of, and adored by her mother and father, and by all other relations as well. Even when her sisters were born, she still held her place as the favourite, and as they grew up they in turn became her willing slaves.

In some ways it was a pity Jewel was so beautiful, because as sometimes happens, she became selfish and vain. She didn't want to work on the farm with her sisters, instead she wished to stay at home and sew, or dance, or go and sit by a pool and look at her own reflection.

The only thing she really enjoyed was going to market. There she went willingly to buy and bargain, and watch the sights, and be admired. Various members of the family went to market two or three at a time, and Jewel nearly always managed to be one of them.

One year a sickness fell on the country, and few people escaped without being ill. The people believed that this sickness must be a punishment for some wrong they had done, and they paid very strict attention to all kinds of observances that might seem very odd to other people. As I have said they had great respect for the crocodile who was believed to be very wise and powerful, and they were in the habit of placing offerings in a certain pool for one famous old fellow who appeared to be the leader of these reptiles.

It so happened that on the next market day Jewel's two sisters had fallen ill of the sickness which was ravaging the countryside, and Jewel was asked to take an offering to the pool.

"But, mother, it's market day. I want to go and buy a comb for my hair!" she protested.

"I'm sorry, my child, but someone must go to the pool. It would be a terrible thing if we didn't make the offering, something dreadful might happen. You can go to the market next time."

After a long argument Jewel, angered at her mother's unusual firmness was forced to take a basket of offerings for the crocodile. She had gone some little distance along the path when she met a friend. "Greetings!" called the friend. "We can go to market together! I heard there are to be some beautiful new combs there this time, and I'm going to get the very best I can."

Now Jewel was really very jealous of this other girl, because she also had some reputation for beauty, and Jewel could not bear to think of her friend flaunting around with a beautiful new comb when she herself had none. They were some distance from the village by now, and with luck no one would ever discover she hadn't gone to the pool with the offerings for the crocodile. So she said not a word, but walked on towards the market.

"What are you bringing to the market this time?" asked her friend.

"Oh, nothing much, my Aunt has most of the stuff today," Jewel answered, and went on to talk of other things. She knew, of course, that the basket contained all the delicacies her mother had been able to collect and that it would be easy to barter them for a very fine comb.

When they arrived Jewel said she had to attend to business, and as soon as her friend was out of sight she began to hunt feverishly for the comb vendor. As soon as she found her she eagerly inspected her wares. One beautifully carved comb instantly caught her fancy.

"Have you another like this?" she enquired after she had feasted her eyes on it. "No, that is the only one," replied the old woman. "I wondered if you had sold another like it, I'd have liked two," said Jewel, trying to be casual. In fact she was burning with anxiety in case there had been two identical ones, and that her friend might have already secured the other one. "No two of my combs are alike," snapped the old lady. "Do you want it or not?" "I rather like it," Jewel said cautiously. "What will you take for it? I have some very nice things in my basket." "Let me see!" commanded the old woman. So Jewel opened her basket, and the two of them began to barter, each trying to beat the other down.

A crowd of amused spectators gathered, Jewel didn't mind this, she was proud of her wit, and was holding her own, but she was dismayed when she saw her friend arrive. Jewel guessed that her friend would desire this very comb.

"Why do you not give her what she asks?" the friend said mischievously. "If you don't think the comb is worth it, I'm willing to offer this very fine jar in exchange!" Now this really was against all the rules because two friends never tried to outbid each other, and Jewel turned and thoroughly abused the other, while the crowd took her side. The girl was forced to slink away, but not before she had noticed the unusual contents of Jewel's basket. "Of course you will get what you want for those things," she snapped. "They are more suitable for an offering than for barter!"

At this Jewel felt her heart sink, but it was too late to back out now, so she hastily concluded the deal, took the comb and started back home. She decided to return by a route that would make it appear that she was coming from the pool, and not from the market.

"You have been a very long time, I was becoming worried," her mother remarked.

"I sat by the pool and forgot that time was passing," Jewel replied.

"Well, will you tend the fire? Our neighbour is ill now, and I must visit her," said the mother. "This illness is indeed terrible, I only hope that the spirits will see fit to be kind, and restore us to health soon."

But the illness spread, and became worse, until one day a meeting was called, and all the village attended.

"There must be a curse on us," an old man quavered. "Some one has offended the Spirits. Will the culprit confess so that he may be punished, and the village will be saved."

There was a great deal of talk of this kind, and many people accused others, and the accused were examined, but nothing was proven against anyone. Then Jewel was horrified to see her friend whispering to one of the old men. While she was trying to make up her mind whether to run away or not, the old fellow raised a great cry.

"The offender has been named," he cried. "It is the girl Jewel. She kept back the offering to the crocodile, and bartered it at the market for a comb!"

Immediately a terrible hubbub arose, and Jewel was forced to stand in the middle of the circle.

"Is this story true?" thundered the Chief.

"Of course it's true!" the jealous girl cried out. "I can vouch for it, and you can prove it yourselves by visiting the comb vendor!"

"It is not true!" Jewel exclaimed. "I have no comb!"

"Then you have hidden it. Let us go, and search her house!" shouted the accuser.

Despite the protests of Jewel, and the lamentations of her mother the crowd hurried towards the house.

"I know where she hides her treasures, under the wall, near the water jar," the false friend shouted gleefully, and rushed to the spot. She found the comb almost at once, and held it up for all to see.

At this the crowd became terribly angry.

"Cast her to the crocodiles," they cried. "That will be fit punishment!"

So Jewel was dragged towards the pool, bound and left to the mercy of the crocodiles.

"Much good may your beauty do you now!" sneered her one time friend.

Now Jewel knew the pool very well, how often she had sat there for hours admiring her reflection, and how often she had watched the crocodile. She was careful, of course, and always ready to rise and run if he came near, but he was a lazy old fellow, well fed with offerings, and never took much notice of her. "He won't bother with me," she assured herself now. "He's too fat, and lazy," but nevertheless when she saw him appearing out of the water, she felt very frightened.

He looked at her with his strange eyes, and it seemed to her that he sneered.

"Well, you've got yourself into a nice mess," he said in a deep, harsh voice.

"You can talk!" Jewel exclaimed.

"Certainly I can talk. I don't often do it of course, so few things are worth talking about!"

"Oh, I'm so glad," Jewel exclaimed. "I'm sorry about your offering. Truly I am. I'd do anything to make up for it, if only you'll use your influence and have the sickness taken from us."

"The sickness is nothing to do with me," said the crocodile. "I didn't cause it, and I can't do anything about taking it away."

"Oh, then it wouldn't have made any difference if I had given you the offering. Oh, this is terrible. My friend has my beautiful comb, and I'm here, and I suppose you'll eat me. Oh how miserable I am!" and she burst into sobs.

"Stop making that horrible noise," snapped the crocodile. "I'm not going to eat you. I'm too old, my teeth aren't what they were; but you are going to be punished!"

"How?" quavered Jewel.

"You are going to stay here!"

"You mean live here by this pool?"

"Yes!"

"But I don't understand. I won't mind doing that for a time!"

"It won't be for a time, it will be for ever. You can look after the offerings they bring me."

"But why?" asked Jewel. "I'll have so little to do, and I'd have nothing to eat."

"You may eat some of the offerings."

Jewel sighed, and was silent. After all she was very lucky. She was not going to be eaten, and she wouldn't mind living at the pool for a time. She couldn't believe it would be for long, because even if the crocodile didn't relent and let her go, she would surely be able to escape.

"May I build myself a shelter?" she enquired.

"You may," said the crocodile, and then proceeded to talk in such guttural tones that Jewel could not understand a word. Startled she looked round, and discovered that a large number of crocodiles of all ages were sitting in a ring behind her. She was so startled that she screamed.

"It's all right," said the crocodile. "They won't hurt you. At least not unless you try to escape."

Jewel felt her heart sink. Was it going to be more difficult to escape than she imagined?

"May I gather reeds for the shelter now?" she quavered.

"Go ahead!" the crocodile told her.

So she wriggled out of her bonds, and when she was free, she made her way to the bank and gathered reeds. A number of young crocodiles followed her. There was no hope of escape. By night she had built a shelter where she slept, and next morning she rose, washed at the edge of the pool, and used it as a mirror while she

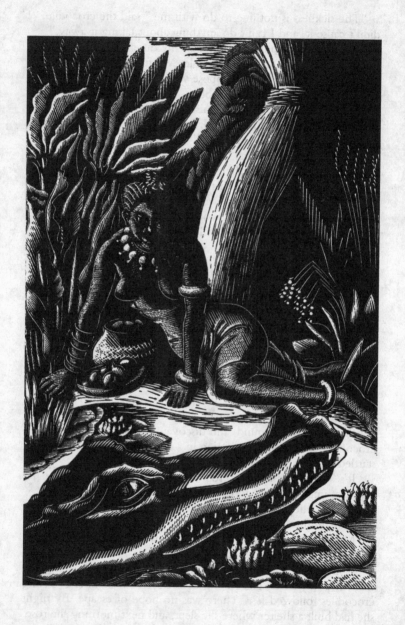

did her toilet. She was glad to see that the events of the past twenty-four hours had not affected her looks, and wished that she had her beautiful comb. It was galling to think of it in the hands of her betrayer.

So the days passed. Jewel fed on the offerings, watched people come and go, although they were afraid to speak to her, and spent much of her time admiring her reflection in the pool. After a while, however, she became bored even with this.

"Why keep me here?" she asked the old crocodile. "Please let me go. I'll do anything if you'll only give me freedom."

"What more do you want?" asked the crocodile. "You are fed, you are comfortable. You don't have to do anything, and you can spend hours gazing at yourself in the pool." He turned and plunged into the water, and Jewel did not see him for a long time.

Time was passing, and still Jewel was a prisoner. Still no one spoke to her, but she heard the people who passed talking between themselves. She heard of marriages among those she knew, girls younger than herself. If she had been free she would probably have been married by now. For the first time Jewel began to think seriously about the future. Suppose the crocodile kept her here until she was an old, old woman. With nothing to do but look at herself in the pool, and gradually she would see her looks change. As the years passed she would see all her youth and beauty fade.

She could think of no more horrible fate, and she felt sure that this was just what the crocodile had planned. She had no idea how long she had been his prisoner, one day was so much like the other that it seemed as if years had passed.

Feeling desperate she decided that she would jump into the pool and drown herself. Fearing that if she stayed to think much about it she would lose courage, she jumped to her feet, shut her eyes, ran towards the pool, and fell down, down into the water. But only for a few minutes. She felt herself seized, and dragged out again.

"Tch, tch," exclaimed the old crocodile, as he set her on the bank. "What is the meaning of this?"

"I'm so miserable I'd rather be dead than stay here any longer," she cried.

"But what displeases you about the life?" asked the crocodile. "Think how you used to leave tasks undone, and creep away here and gaze at your own reflection for hours. Now you can do it all the time."

"I don't want to. I'm sick of my own reflection," Jewel sobbed. "Besides if I stay here my reflection will change, I'll get old and ugly and I don't want to look at myself when I'm old and ugly."

"What do you want to do?" asked the crocodile.

"I want to go back home and live like an ordinary girl."

"But you never did live like an ordinary girl. You lived the life of a very spoiled girl," the crocodile reminded her. "You treated your sisters as if they were your slaves. You never helped your mother. You never did any useful work."

"I was foolish," Jewel exclaimed. "I don't know why I was so foolish. All I want now is to live like anyone else, I'll gladly work. I'm sick of having nothing to do all day!"

The crocodile closed his eyes, and thought for some time.

"All right," he said at last. "I'll let you go, but on conditions. You must work as you say you wish to do, and you must bring me an offering every day, and if ever I catch you dawdling over the pool admiring yourself, I shall surely eat you, even though I have few teeth, and will probably suffer agonies of indigestion. Now go!"

Thankfully Jewel rose to her feet, gasped out her thanks, and ran down the track that led to the village.

Her poor mother was delighted to see her back Only fear of what punishment might fall on the village had kept her from going to her daughter. No one else rejoiced particularly, they didn't care much one way or another. The affair was months old, the sickness had gone, and they had other matters to interest them.

Jewel, however, was a changed girl. She worked long, and hard, and daily she made her way to the pool with offerings, until she was an old, old woman, and no one remembered anything about the story except a few old people like herself and, of course, the old crocodile who looked much the same, and probably does to this day.

THE MAN-IN-THE-MOON
AND HIS WIFE

LONG, LONG AGO, the man-in-the-moon and his wife Atai, had a quarrel which led to very strange results. These two were the royalty of the skies once the sun had gone down. The man you all know, he looked then as he does now. Sometimes he was smiling, sometimes he looked grim. His wife was the greatest and brightest of the stars, all the other stars were her servants. When she came out they grouped themselves round her, and secretly they thought she was just as splendid as the moon, and that she was very much more useful, and that they were also.

They had some reason on their side, for sailors guided their ships by the position of the stars, and many wise men believed they could foretell the future by studying them. This included not only events of great importance, but the future of human beings according to the stars that were shining when they were born. The moon on the other hand could only travel through the heavens and shed light.

After some time the man-in-the-moon began to hear whispers of all this, and he became jealous. He had been shining long before people thought of building ships, or foretelling the future, or didn't like these new fangled notions which threatened his supremacy. So he became very angry, and decided not to shine at all, or to allow the stars to shine either. In order to prevent them doing this he sought the support of some of the elements. He

143

sought out the rain, and thunder and lightning. "The stars are becoming conceited," he told them. "They think they have command of the heavens, and they have to be taught better!" After a good deal of talk of this kind he persuaded the elements to do their worst. The rain poured down, thunder crashed, and lightning flashed. The earth darkened, the rivers were flooded and over-ran the earth. Trees were swept away, low lying country was over-whelmed with water, animals and birds were drowned, and the people of the earth were driven into caves and on tops of high mountains, where they led the most miserable existence.

Days passed in this way. The people starved and froze because even the sun could not make any impression on the deluge, and it seemed as if the whole world must be destroyed. The man-in-the-moon didn't care, however. He retired well content because his wife and the other stars couldn't shine.

Atai was furious, and sulked, and vowed that the deluge could go on for ever as far as she was concerned. Her husband had prevented her shining, but he couldn't shine himself either. In fact being idle didn't improve either of their tempers, while the stormy elements who had never had control over the world before, were thoroughly enjoying their power.

Down below, man, the unfortunate victim of this celestial quarrel, was in terrible straits. He prayed and made sacrifices, and everyone blamed everyone else for offending the Gods, and as a result people began to quarrel and make war among themselves. Their troubles were increased by the fact that they were preyed upon by wild animals, and had to keep great fires burning in the caves to frighten the beasts. At night, beyond the ring of fire, men could see the eyes of fierce lions, tigers, and wolves, waiting to attack them. This was not because lions, tigers and wolves preferred to eat men, they did not, but the animals they usually stalked were becoming more and more scarce.

At length the little stars became very perturbed at the deadlock. They approached Atai and petitioned her to abandon the quarrel. They suggested that there should be some agreement between the moon and the stars. When the moon was at his brightest the stars could remain in the background, and when the moon had retired the stars could have the heavens to themselves. They pointed out that if the stormy elements continued to hold power, there would be no light on earth, and that indeed after a time there would be no earth left.

Atai, who was by this time very bored with the quarrel, at first pretended indifference about what happened in the future, but eventually the little stars persuaded her to allow them to go to the man-in-the-moon, and make peace offers. Their reception was better than they expected because he was in no way happy about his own position. He wasn't ruling the heavens, and he had lost his wife. When the little stars put their suggestions before him, of course, he had to pretend a certain amount of indifference.

"I am very glad that you come in this spirit," he informed them. "It cannot be disputed that I am the real ruler, but I do not wish this foolish quarrel to continue. For my own part, I am prepared to remain in retirement, but I feel I have responsibilities to the earth. If the present state of affairs continues the earth will be ruined."

The little stars enthusiastically supported this view, and were very complimentary about his unselfish spirit. They then went into possible terms of settlement, and after a great deal of discussion the moon agreed. It was arranged that the new plan should start forthwith. But the man-in-the-moon found himself with another problem on his hands. The elements having been given control were not prepared to abandon it. Finally, a three-cornered agreement had to be made. Sometimes the moon would shine and the stars would be comparatively dim. When the moon retired the stars would come out in their full splendour, but there was to be a third period when there was complete darkness with rain and storms.

The man-in-the-moon and his wife patched up their quarrel, and have remained on the best of terms ever since. Some people consider that there is nothing more beautiful than a full moon slipping across the skies, others love the splendour of the stars. Wise men write books about them, sailors navigate by them, and astrologers claim to read the future in the starlit heavens. But no one is happy when rain and storms sweep the earth. Gentle rain is welcomed, of course, but not the floods, and thunder and lightning, but man has had to accept them, for they come as regularly as night and day. In the rainy season man has to take cover and exist as best he can until the storms pass, and the fine weather returns once more.

BATS DON'T BELONG

THE BATS WERE the busiest creatures in the forest, for the bats had plans. No one was quite sure where the bats had come from, or in fact *why* bats were. They weren't even sure of it themselves. They could both fly and creep. Many of them believed they could fly even better than the birds. The ones with large, strong wings were very proud of themselves. Then there were others who were as strong as some of the animals, and the animals were afraid of them.

It seemed to the bats that they were getting somewhere. Most of the other creatures of the forest could have traced their ancestors back through the dim ages, and the ancestors would have appeared little different to their descendants if they had come back to earth. The birds and animals were bound by ancient settled habits, and they belonged either to the earth or the air, but the bats had the freedom of both domains, they resembled mice or rats with their own airplanes. In their secret hearts it seemed to the bats that they might one day be lords of both earth and air. For this reason they were very concerned with their own affairs, and didn't notice much of what was going on around them.

And there were strange happenings. For one thing there was a drought, and almost everyone was bad tempered as a result. As always when there is trouble an effort was made to hold *somebody* responsible. Food was short, so the animals blamed the birds for eating too much. The birds accused the animals of meanness, and others of hoarding, and feeling ran higher and higher. Quarrels broke out.

The first thing the bats knew about it was when the Leader, out on his usual nocturnal hunt, bumped into a large owl.

"Hello! What are you doing here?" squeaked the Bat Leader.

"I'm watching. Haven't you heard that the animals who used to sleep all night, now rove round, and steal our food. It's my job to keep a look-out and raise the alarm!"

"Steal your food!" echoed the bat.

"Well, everybody's food. You know how short things are. We've tried to enforce a sort of rationing scheme. We—well, almost all of us, have kept our word, but the animals are sneaking round at night eating more than they should. If we catch them there is going to be trouble."

"What will you do?"

"We'll fight!" The owl ruffled his feathers until he looked like a huge puff-ball and glared in the most menacing way.

The bat didn't like any of this. He was a peaceful fellow, and didn't want to be bothered with other people's troubles. As he and his fellows only hunted for food for a few brief hours of the night, always had done so, and couldn't do anything else on account of poor eyesight, he felt this new trouble was no affair of his. So he bade the owl farewell and flitted on.

On his way home he was amazed to see a lion sitting outside his cave, very much on the alert. He was accustomed to seeing lions stalking prey in the moonlight, but this was something different.

"Hello," squeaked the bat. "Aren't you going to bed?"

"Not till after sunrise," growled the lion. "Then the elephant takes over. You see we have to keep guard over our food because of those unscrupulous birds. Since the shortage came they have turned completely dishonest. So I keep watch and roar if I see any of them flying round. If they persist, there is going to be a very serious situation. We animals are peaceful folk, but there are limits to our patience."

The bat went home to bed in a thoughtful mood. If this went on it looked like war.

A few days later war was declared. War between the animals and the birds. The animals had demanded that the birds keep to the trees and never descend to the earth, and the birds maintained that they had a perfect right to either sphere, and were not going to give up their rights.

The bats decided that all this was nothing to do with them, and declared themselves neutral. They went about their business as usual, and were perfectly polite and friendly with both sides.

Naturally this soon made them unpopular. Because they spoke to the birds, the animals decided they were spies carrying information to their feathered friends. The birds in turn suspected them of giving away secrets to the animals. Everything became more and more difficult for the bats, and they found themselves having to retreat further and further into their caves in order to keep out of trouble.

Meanwhile, the war went on. At first the birds suffered the worst casualties. On the other hand they could rove further for their food at greater speed than could the animals. Some of the animals starved to death, and then an epidemic started, and animals died in large numbers. For this reason it seemed to the animals that they had better get hold of all the allies they could, and so diplomatic approaches were made to the bats. A large rat was sent along to discuss matters with the leader of the bats.

"We feel that for your own sake, you should be on our side," he pointed out. "After all, you are far more animal than bird, you are bound to us by old ties and associations. If we are beaten you will be completely at the mercy of the birds. We stand for the order that has served the forest for so long. Everyone in his place, and everyone getting a fair share. The birds will destroy all that if they get into power."

The Bat Leader looked thoughtful. This was the first time the animals had claimed such close kinship with the bats. Things must be pretty bad, for up to the present the animals had shown the bats small consideration. In fact there had been several regrettable incidents, during which bats had been attacked and killed. The excuse always was, of course, that the bat had been mistaken for a bird.

The Leader, therefore, squeaked non-committal answers.

"This is a very serious matter for us. We are pacifist on principle. We don't believe in wars. However, we shall give you an answer in due course when the matter has had our full consideration."

"How soon will that be?" the rat asked suspiciously.

"Not for a little time, I'm afraid; You see so many of my people have gone to attend to the fruit crop in the South. We must have our fair share, and then the new colony just settled in those splendid caves we've discovered in Calabar, have a great deal to do at present."

The rat swished his tail in irritation, but there was nothing he could do but make a polite answer, and go away quietly. He had been especially warned not to lose his temper.

The Bat Leader was swinging cosily from his favourite perch on the roof of the cave, when a small bat came to inform him that some special emissaries from the bird world had come to see him. Having kept them waiting for ten minutes the Leader descended and went to the mouth of the cave.

The emissaries looked impressive at first glance. A gorgeous flamingo, an imposing pelican, and an eloquent, brilliantly hued parrot. But the Leader noticed that they were all very thin, and he felt sure they would have given every feather they possessed for a really good meal.

After polite exchanges the parrot got down to business.

"We shall be frank with you, brother. This war is going badly. We think the time has come to warn you of your own danger if you keep neutral. This is a war of the old order against the new. We stand for freedom, freedom of the earth for everybody. If the animals win they will keep us to the tree tops, and it will only be a matter of time before they keep you there as well. If you value your liberty, you must come in on our side. After all, you are our kinsman. You are far more bird than beast."

The Bat Leader tried to look profound. He was perfectly well aware that the birds were doing badly, but then the animals were doing badly too, and the epidemic was killing them off. Squeaking lengthily, he said so much, and in such an obscure way, that at the end of it the birds didn't really know what he thought, nor was he any too sure himself. However, he got rid of them at last and returned home to call a meeting.

The real point was, did the bats belong to the bird world or the animal world? Some bats held one view, and some the other, while a third party maintained that they were superior people far above either birds or beasts. Time passed, and the discussion went on, also the war went on, and the birds and animals continued to die.

Then one day the sky became overcast. A few drops of rain fell; torrents of rain fell. It rained so hard that the war had to be abandoned, and everyone had to take shelter. Thousands of refugees from both sides arrived in the caves of the bats. Finally the rain grew less, but all over the forest streams trickled. Grass began to grow, food became more plentiful. Everyone was so thirsty and so hungry that they began to eat all they could, and the war was forgotten. In the end there was an armistice.

Nearly all this passed over the heads of the bats because they continued to argue as to whether they were birds or animals. The question was never properly settled. It never has been to this day. Everyone argues about it, including learned men all over the world, but no one can completely decide. Because of this bats don't belong either to the birds or the animals, and neither side wants to claim kinship with them. But they are very self sufficient folk and they don't seem to mind.

NEVER ANGRY

VERY FEW OF us are as good tempered as we might be, although we often wish that we were. On the other hand the person who is always good tempered has troubles also. Once there was a little girl whose good temper was known to everyone. When she was a baby she was never peevish, and scarcely ever cried. This earned her the name, "Never Angry," and no one ever called her anything else.

The baby grew up, but she never fought or quarrelled as other children did. When her companions realised this they began to appreciate it. True, at first they just teased her to see if they could make her cross, but they didn't succeed. So they stopped and sometimes they even made efforts to imitate her, but they weren't very successful. At some time or other something happened to make everyone lose his temper, everyone that is, but Never Angry.

Now one reason why Never Angry was like this, was that her mother had a bad temper, and this made life so unpleasant that Never Angry had firmly resolved that she would never make herself and others unhappy through ill-humour. As she grew up it was only natural that her daughter's character, far from pleasing the mother, should irritate her, because it seemed like a constant reproach to herself.

152

"Why can't you be like other people," she stormed at the girl. "You are deliberately pretending to be good humoured in order to seem better than everyone else!"

"But if I never feel cross why should I pretend that I do?" Never Angry asked reasonably.

"You would often feel cross if your life was as hard as mine," the mother retorted. "Here you are an only child. It's easy for you to have a sunny disposition. You have no worries."

"Perhaps so," said the girl, and began to tidy up the house, because in truth the mother was one of those people who was so constantly upset by worries over trifles, and imaginary slights, or fancied illnesses, that the house was pretty much neglected.

As the years passed the mother made life more and more difficult for the daughter. Secretly she never ceased to exert herself to try and upset the girl's serenity. She made jibes at her, repeated remarks which were supposed to have been made by her friends, and deliberately inflicted all sorts of small hardships, and petty annoyances. But it was all useless, Never Angry went her way quietly, and sometimes looked at her mother as if she were sorry for her, as indeed she was.

She herself was never really unhappy, although she might well have been for her life at home was not pleasant, and although she was really a very pretty girl, she had none of the small things that her companions were given to help them look their best. Her clothes were very poor, and her mother never gave her presents.

One day the mother felt she could not stand her daughter's calm any longer. The girl's godmother lived in a distant place, and sometimes lent them a little money. Previously the mother had always gone on these borrowing missions herself, but this time she decided to send her daughter. It was a long, difficult, and even dangerous journey. "Let's see if she will keep her temper when she finds herself alone in the bush, stung by flies, or when she tries to get across that piece of swamp!" the mother said to herself.

So next day she sent the girl off, with very little food, and instructions that she was not to come back without some money. Never Angry much disliked being sent on such an errand, but as usual she remained good humoured about it, and went quietly.

Now because Never Angry didn't get cross, naturally she never wanted to do anyone any harm, and therefore it never occurred to her that anyone might want to harm her. So when she came upon a great chimpanzee sitting right in the middle of her path, she simply went straight on, and asked very politely if she might pass.

This chimpanzee, who was the terror of the particular piece of forest in which he lived, was naturally very annoyed at this girl who showed no fear of him. Usually humans took one look at him and fled, and the fact that this one did no such thing was most upsetting.

"Who are you?" he roared.

"My name is Never Angry," the girl replied.

"That's a silly name. What do they call you that for?"

"Because I never get angry!"

"And what good does that do?" snorted the chimpanzee.

"I don't know, but if I don't feel angry, why should I pretend to be?"

"Because if you don't you'll be put upon," the big monkey assured her. "Where are you going, anyhow?"

Never Angry told him about the journey on which her mother had sent her.

"Hm, didn't I tell you you'd be put on. You are a bit of a fool you know. Aren't you frightened?"

"Of what?" asked Never Angry.

"Of what might happen—of me for instance?"

"Why, no," the girl told him with composure. "Why should I be? I wouldn't hurt you, so why should you hurt me?"

At this the chimpanzee bellowed with laughter until tears ran down his cheeks.

"So you wouldn't hurt me!" he roared. "That's a good one!" and off he went into another gale of laughter.

"And you never get cross?" he asked as he wiped his eyes.

"No!"

At this the chimpanzee looked cunning, and then began to tease, and bait the girl in order to rouse her temper. But it was no use. She had lived too long with her mother not to know all the moves in this game. So she simply made calm and reasonable answers to all his sallies, until he gave up.

"Well," the monkey said at last, "You certainly live up to your name. You'd better go on your way now, or you'll be late. Good luck!"

Never Angry thanked him and went on. Further along the path a lion spied her coming, and was so annoyed at her intrusion that he leapt out into her path hoping to frighten her.

"Who are you?" he roared.

The girl told him her name, and the lion roared again. "Never Angry! What nonsense. I'll make you angry," and he seized her playfully and mauled her round in the dust, but she only waited passively until he had done. She knew he wouldn't find it much fun to play with someone who didn't put up a fight.

After a moment or two the lion desisted, and looked down at her. "Well," he said, "you certainly deserve your name. Here, brush yourself down with the end of my tail, and wipe your face in my mane. That's right. Now you'd better get along, and you have my blessing. I wish all human beings were like you."

So Never Angry went on until she came to a place where the path was very narrow, and here curled up, and eyeing her evilly, was a large python. "Please, may I pass?" she asked him.

The python was almost struck dumb for a moment, because never before had any human being come up and spoken politely to him, without any trace of anger or fear.

"Who are you?" he stammered at last. "What are you doing here? You have no right to be on this piece of path, it's mine!"

"I am Never Angry!"

"I don't care whether you are never angry or not, I simply asked your name, and where you are going!"

"My name is Never Angry!"

"How idiotic. I have never heard anything so silly in my life. Everyone gets angry sometimes. I do myself, and I'm a singularly amiable fellow."

"I don't get angry, I don't know what it is to feel angry," the girl replied.

"Then there must be something the matter with you, that is if you are telling the truth. Let's see, shall we?"

At that the python slid over, and made her a prisoner in his coils. "Now I'll keep you here, and find out how you really feel," the python went on.

Never Angry gave a small sigh, and then remained still, and unruffled, until at last the puzzled python released her.

"Well," he said, "I see you were telling me the truth, but I think you're likely to get yourself into trouble all the same."

"But why?" the girl asked quietly. "You are the third person I've met on the way and in each case we've parted good friends."

"Well, maybe, you're right," the python said grudgingly. "Anyhow the village isn't far from here, and so you ought to get there safely enough. Go with my blessing."

So Never Angry bid the snake farewell, and walked on into the village, and went in search of her godmother. Although she did not know it Never Angry's godmother was no ordinary woman, she could work magic, and sometimes she did it to punish the wicked, and sometimes to reward the good. She was very interested when she heard the girl's story.

"Why did not your mother come herself?" she asked.

So Never Angry told her how her mother held the belief that she, Never Angry, was good tempered simply because it was not difficult to be good tempered when all went well, and life was easy.

"And was it easy to come here?" asked the Godmother.

"It was really, because I met so many good friends on the way," Never Angry replied, and went on to tell about the chimpanzee, and the lion, and the snake. Secretly the Godmother was amazed at this story and wondered if it could really be true. However, she asked no questions, but resolved to find out the truth in her own way. So she asked the girl in, and kept her for some days. During those days she secretly put her to many tests, and discovered it was true. In all difficulties Never Angry remained serene and reasonable.

At last the Godmother called the girl to her, and told her she would now send her home.

"You have all my blessings," she said. "Because I find you are well named, and you are a good, kind girl. Don't worry about the journey back, and don't worry about the future, for I think I can promise you that it is going to be very different to the past. I am not going to send you back as you came, and we shall have a feast before you go. Now you are going to see how beautiful you can be!"

At this the Godmother clapped her hands, and three hand-maidens appeared and they led the girl away, and bathed her in perfumed water until her skin was clear and beautiful. Then they washed, and dressed her hair, and after that they attired her in wonderful new clothes. Then they led her back and there was a wonderful farewell feast waiting for her.

At the end of the feast the Godmother raised her hands for silence. "I am going to send this beautiful girl home now. What wind will volunteer to carry her?"

At this a blustering wind arose and almost knocked everyone off their feet. "No, no," cried the Godmother. "This girl must travel on a gentle wind!" So the rough wind went away and a gentle one blew up instead. Then the Godmother bid Never Angry farewell, having put a small bag with money, and a large bag with new clothes in her hands. Never Angry found herself floating up gently, leaving the earth below, and gliding softly over the tree tops.

When the sun became warm she found herself floating down until she reached the bank of a beautiful river where she bathed, and then the wind wafted her on once more.

In the evening she found herself outside her own village, and she walked towards her mother's house looking so radiantly beautiful that everyone stopped to stare.

When the mother saw her daughter arriving home looking so beautiful, so wonderfully dressed, and so free from the stains and fatigues of travel, she was astounded.

Never Angry handed her mother the money.

"And how did you come by these clothes?" the mother enquired. "Have you been spending some of the money on them? They cost a pretty penny."

Never Angry explained gently that her Godmother had given them to her.

Then the mother questioned her daughter about all that had happened on the journey, and what it was like in the Godmother's house.

"I'm sure you have lost your temper many times since you set out from home?" she said bitterly.

Never Angry said she had not, and proceeded to tell how kind everyone had been. As she talked the mother realised how badly she had behaved to her daughter. She seemed to hear the voice of the Godmother in her ears telling her how lucky she was to have such an unusual child, and that she should cherish, and not punish her.

"You have done well," the mother said at last. "I am proud of you. I am beginning to think you are right after all, and in future we shall try to live your way. I shall never be angry either."

Of course the mother didn't really succeed in this fine resolve but she did keep her temper much better than before, and later on, when her beautiful daughter made a fine marriage, it was much easier for her to do this. As for Never Angry she became famous all through the country, and was often called upon to give advice and make judgments, because she was never angry, and never afraid.

Many people tried to follow her example besides her mother, and they didn't do so badly. There were fewer quarrels and disputes in her country than in the past so that everyone became more secure and more prosperous than they had ever been before.